TEACHER'S PET PUBLICATIONS

PUZZLE PACK
for
Othello

based on the play by
William Shakespeare

Written by
William T. Collins

© 2005 Teacher's Pet Publications
All Rights Reserved

The materials in this packet are copyrighted
by Teacher's Pet Publications, Inc.

These pages may be duplicated by the purchaser
for use in the purchaser's own classroom.

Copying any of these materials and distributing them
for any other purpose is a violation of the copyright laws.

© 2005 Teacher's Pet Publications, Inc.
www.tpet.com

INTRODUCTION
If you already own the LitPlan for this title, this Puzzle Pack will refresh your Unit Resource Materials and Vocabulary Resource Materials sections plus give you additional materials you can substitute into the tests. If you do not already have a complete LitPlan, these pages will give you some supplemental materials to use with your own plan. There are two main groups of materials: one set for unit words (such as characters' names, symbols, places, etc.) and one set for vocabulary words associated with the book.

WORD LIST
There is a word list for both the unit words and the vocabulary words. These lists show you which words are being used in the materials and the clues or definitions being used for those words. You may want to give students a word list with clues/definitions to help them, or you may want students to only have a word list (without clues/definitions) if you want them to work a little harder. Both are available for duplication. The word lists can also be your "calling key" for the bingo games.

FILL IN THE BLANK AND MATCHING
There are 4 each of the fill in the blank and matching worksheets for both the unit and vocabulary words. These pages can be used either as extra worksheets for students or as objective parts of a unit test. They can be done individually if students need extra help or as a whole class activity to review the material covered.

MAGIC SQUARES
The magic squares not only reinforce the material covered but also work on reasoning and math skills. Many teachers have told us that their students really enjoy doing these!

WORD SEARCH PUZZLES
The word search words go in all directions, as indicated on your answer keys. Two of the word search puzzles have the clues listed rather than the words. This makes the puzzle a little more difficult, but it reinforces the material better. Two word search puzzles have words only for students who find the clue puzzles too difficult.

CROSSWORD PUZZLES
Both unit and vocabulary word sections have 4 crossword puzzles.

BINGO CARDS
There are 32 individual bingo cards for the unit words and 32 individual bingo cards for the vocabulary words. You can use your word list as a "call list," calling the words at random and marking them off of your list as you go, or you could use the flash cards by cutting them apart and drawing the words at random from a hat (or box or whatever). To make a better review, you might ask for the definition and spelling of each word as you call it out–or you could call out the definitions and have students tell you the words they need to look for on the puzzle.

JUGGLE LETTERS
The vocabulary juggle letter game is intended to help students learn the spellings of the words. One sheet has the definitions listed on it as an extra help for students who need it or to reinforce the definitions if you choose to do so.

FLASH CARDS
We've included a set of vocabulary flash cards you can duplicate, cut, and fold for your students. Some teachers make a few sets for general use by the class; others make a set for each student. Some teachers duplicate them for each student and have the students cut & fold their own. You can cut out just the words and put them in a hat, have each student pick out one word and write the definition and a sentence for that word. Students then swap words and papers, with the next student adding a sentence of his own under the last one. You can have students swap as many times as you like. Each time the student will read the sentences written prior to his own and then add a sentence. You can cut out the words and definitions separately and play "I Have; Who Has?" Each student in the room draws a word and definition. The first student says, "I have (the name of the word). Who has the definition?" The student with the definition reads it then says, "I have (the name of the vocabulary word she has). Who has the definition?" The round continues until all words and definitions have been given.

Othello Word List

No.	Word	Clue/Definition
1.	ACT	Play division
2.	AM	'I ___ not what I ___.'
3.	BIANCA	Cassio's mistress
4.	BRABANTIO	Desdemona's father
5.	CASSIO	Becomes Lord Governor at the end of the play
6.	CONFESSED	Iago's actions ___ his guilt.
7.	DESDEMONA	Othello's wife
8.	DIE	'Yet she must ___, else she'll betray more men.'
9.	DOG	'Oh, damned Iago! Oh, inhuman ___!'
10.	DREAM	Iago lied & told Othello Cassio had a ___ in which he cried out to Desdemona.
11.	EMILIA	Iago's wife; Desdemona's servant
12.	FRIENDSHIP	Othello's ___ with Iago keeps him from questioning Iago's loyalty.
13.	GRATIANO	Brother of Brabantio
14.	HANDKERCHIEF	Personal item belonging to Desdemona; Othello thinks she gave it to Cassio
15.	HATE	'For naught did I in ___, but all in honor.'
16.	HONESTY	'So please your Grace, my Ancient, a man he is of ___ and trust....'
17.	HUSBAND	Othello to Desdemona
18.	IAGO	He was passed over for promotion.
19.	INNOCENT	Emilia said Desdemona was ___.
20.	JEALOUSY	Motive for Othello's actions
21.	JUDGEMENT	'... yet that I put the Moor At least into a jealousy so strong that ___ cannot cure.'
22.	KNAVERY	'...___'s plain face is never seen till used.'
23.	LETTERS	These, found in Roderigo's pockets, were evidence against Iago.
24.	LIES	Iago told lots of these.
25.	LODOVICO	Tells of the letter found in Roderigo's pockets
26.	LOYALTY	Emilia's ___ to Iago proves stronger than her ___ to Desdemona.
27.	MOOR	Othello's heritage
28.	MURDER	Iago plots to ___ Cassio
29.	NET	'And out of her own goodness make the ___ that shall enmesh them all.'
30.	NOBODY	'___, I myself. Farewell.'
31.	NOSE	'The Moor ... will as tenderly be led by the ___ As asses are.'
32.	OTHELLO	The jealous Moor
33.	PLAN	Plot; scheme
34.	REPUTATION	'___, ___, ___! Oh, I have lost my ___!'
35.	REVENGE	Iago's motive
36.	RODERIGO	He is love-sick for Desdemona.
37.	SCENE	Act division
38.	SEEM	'Men should be what they ___.'
39.	SHAKESPEARE	Author William
40.	STABS	Othello ___ himself and dies.
41.	VIRTUE	'So I will turn her ___ into pitch....'
42.	WEB	'There's magic in the ___ of it.'
43.	WIFE	Emilia to Iago
44.	WORK	'___ on, My medicine, ___!'
45.	YEARS	'...you shall more command with ___ Than with your weapons.'

Othello Fill In The Blanks 1

_____

_____

_____

_____

_____

_____

_____

_____

_____

_____

_____

_____

_____

_____

_____

_____

_____

_____

_____

_____

1. 'There's magic in the ___ of it.'
2. Iago lied & told Othello Cassio had a ___ in which he cried out to Desdemona.
3. Personal item belonging to Desdemona; Othello thinks she gave it to Cassio
4. Brother of Brabantio
5. The jealous Moor
6. Iago's wife; Desdemona's servant
7. 'And out of her own goodness make the ___ that shall enmesh them all.'
8. Cassio's mistress
9. Othello to Desdemona
10. '___, I myself. Farewell.'
11. 'Men should be what they ___.'
12. 'So please your Grace, my Ancient, a man he is of ___ and trust....'
13. Iago told lots of these.
14. '... yet that I put the Moor At least into a jealousy so strong that ___ cannot cure.'
15. '...___'s plain face is never seen till used.'
16. 'Yet she must ___, else she'll betray more men.'
17. Act division
18. '...you shall more command with ___ Than with your weapons.'
19. 'So I will turn her ___ into pitch....'
20. Othello's wife

Othello Fill In The Blanks 1 Answer Key

WEB	1. 'There's magic in the ___ of it.'
DREAM	2. Iago lied & told Othello Cassio had a ___ in which he cried out to Desdemona.
HANDKERCHIEF	3. Personal item belonging to Desdemona; Othello thinks she gave it to Cassio
GRATIANO	4. Brother of Brabantio
OTHELLO	5. The jealous Moor
EMILIA	6. Iago's wife; Desdemona's servant
NET	7. 'And out of her own goodness make the ___ that shall enmesh them all.'
BIANCA	8. Cassio's mistress
HUSBAND	9. Othello to Desdemona
NOBODY	10. '___, I myself. Farewell.'
SEEM	11. 'Men should be what they ___.'
HONESTY	12. 'So please your Grace, my Ancient, a man he is of ___ and trust....'
LIES	13. Iago told lots of these.
JUDGEMENT	14. '... yet that I put the Moor At least into a jealousy so strong that ___ cannot cure.'
KNAVERY	15. '...___'s plain face is never seen till used.'
DIE	16. 'Yet she must ___, else she'll betray more men.'
SCENE	17. Act division
YEARS	18. '...you shall more command with ___ Than with your weapons.'
VIRTUE	19. 'So I will turn her ___ into pitch....'
DESDEMONA	20. Othello's wife

Othello Fill In The Blanks 2

_____

1. 'Oh, damned Iago! Oh, inhuman ___!'
2. 'I ___ not what I ___.'
3. Othello ___ himself and dies.
4. Play division
5. '___, I myself. Farewell.'
6. Iago plots to ___ Cassio
7. The jealous Moor
8. 'There's magic in the ___ of it.'
9. He was passed over for promotion.
10. Iago's actions ___ his guilt.
11. '___ on, My medicine, ___!'
12. Iago's motive
13. '...___'s plain face is never seen till used.'
14. Motive for Othello's actions
15. He is love-sick for Desdemona.
16. Tells of the letter found in Roderigo's pockets
17. 'Men should be what they ___.'
18. Personal item belonging to Desdemona; Othello thinks she gave it to Cassio
19. Othello's ___ with Iago keeps him from questioning Iago's loyalty.
20. 'And out of her own goodness make the ___ that shall enmesh them all.'

Othello Fill In The Blanks 2 Answer Key

DOG	1. 'Oh, damned Iago! Oh, inhuman ___!'
AM	2. 'I ___ not what I ___.'
STABS	3. Othello ___ himself and dies.
ACT	4. Play division
NOBODY	5. '___, I myself. Farewell.'
MURDER	6. Iago plots to ___ Cassio
OTHELLO	7. The jealous Moor
WEB	8. 'There's magic in the ___ of it.'
IAGO	9. He was passed over for promotion.
CONFESSED	10. Iago's actions ___ his guilt.
WORK	11. '___ on, My medicine, ___!'
REVENGE	12. Iago's motive
KNAVERY	13. '...___'s plain face is never seen till used.'
JEALOUSY	14. Motive for Othello's actions
RODERIGO	15. He is love-sick for Desdemona.
LODOVICO	16. Tells of the letter found in Roderigo's pockets
SEEM	17. 'Men should be what they ___.'
HANDKERCHIEF	18. Personal item belonging to Desdemona; Othello thinks she gave it to Cassio
FRIENDSHIP	19. Othello's ___ with Iago keeps him from questioning Iago's loyalty.
NET	20. 'And out of her own goodness make the ___ that shall enmesh them all.'

Othello Fill In The Blanks 3

_____   1. Iago's motive

_____   2. '___, ___, ___! Oh, I have lost my ___!'

_____   3. 'And out of her own goodness make the ___ that shall enmesh them all.'

_____   4. Emilia said Desdemona was ___.

_____   5. Emilia to Iago

_____   6. 'Men should be what they ___.'

_____   7. Author William

_____   8. Othello's wife

_____   9. 'So please your Grace, my Ancient, a man he is of ___ and trust....'

_____   10. '...___'s plain face is never seen till used.'

_____   11. He is love-sick for Desdemona.

_____   12. Personal item belonging to Desdemona; Othello thinks she gave it to Cassio

_____   13. Act division

_____   14. Othello's ___ with Iago keeps him from questioning Iago's loyalty.

_____   15. Iago's actions ___ his guilt.

_____   16. Iago's wife; Desdemona's servant

_____   17. '... yet that I put the Moor At least into a jealousy so strong that ___ cannot cure.'

_____   18. Iago plots to ___ Cassio

_____   19. Cassio's mistress

_____   20. Becomes Lord Governor at the end of the play

9
Copyrighted

Othello Fill In The Blanks 3 Answer Key

REVENGE	1. Iago's motive
REPUTATION	2. '___, ___, ___! Oh, I have lost my ___!'
NET	3. 'And out of her own goodness make the ___ that shall enmesh them all.'
INNOCENT	4. Emilia said Desdemona was ___.
WIFE	5. Emilia to Iago
SEEM	6. 'Men should be what they ___.'
SHAKESPEARE	7. Author William
DESDEMONA	8. Othello's wife
HONESTY	9. 'So please your Grace, my Ancient, a man he is of ___ and trust....'
KNAVERY	10. '...___'s plain face is never seen till used.'
RODERIGO	11. He is love-sick for Desdemona.
HANDKERCHIEF	12. Personal item belonging to Desdemona; Othello thinks she gave it to Cassio
SCENE	13. Act division
FRIENDSHIP	14. Othello's ___ with Iago keeps him from questioning Iago's loyalty.
CONFESSED	15. Iago's actions ___ his guilt.
EMILIA	16. Iago's wife; Desdemona's servant
JUDGEMENT	17. '... yet that I put the Moor At least into a jealousy so strong that ___ cannot cure.'
MURDER	18. Iago plots to ___ Cassio
BIANCA	19. Cassio's mistress
CASSIO	20. Becomes Lord Governor at the end of the play

Othello Fill In The Blanks 4

_____

1. Tells of the letter found in Roderigo's pockets
2. '___ on, My medicine, ___!'
3. He is love-sick for Desdemona.
4. 'So I will turn her ___ into pitch....'
5. 'And out of her own goodness make the ___ that shall enmesh them all.'
6. Act division
7. He was passed over for promotion.
8. Iago lied & told Othello Cassio had a ___ in which he cried out to Desdemona.
9. Desdemona's father
10. 'For naught did I in ___, but all in honor.'
11. '...you shall more command with ___ Than with your weapons.'
12. '... yet that I put the Moor At least into a jealousy so strong that ___ cannot cure.'
13. Iago's motive
14. Brother of Brabantio
15. Emilia said Desdemona was ___.
16. Emilia's ___ to Iago proves stronger than her ___ to Desdemona.
17. '___, ___, ___! Oh, I have lost my ___!'
18. The jealous Moor
19. Iago told lots of these.
20. Motive for Othello's actions

Othello Fill In The Blanks 4 Answer Key

LODOVICO	1. Tells of the letter found in Roderigo's pockets
WORK	2. '___ on, My medicine, ___!'
RODERIGO	3. He is love-sick for Desdemona.
VIRTUE	4. 'So I will turn her ___ into pitch....'
NET	5. 'And out of her own goodness make the ___ that shall enmesh them all.'
SCENE	6. Act division
IAGO	7. He was passed over for promotion.
DREAM	8. Iago lied & told Othello Cassio had a ___ in which he cried out to Desdemona.
BRABANTIO	9. Desdemona's father
HATE	10. 'For naught did I in ___, but all in honor.'
YEARS	11. '...you shall more command with ___ Than with your weapons.'
JUDGEMENT	12. '... yet that I put the Moor At least into a jealousy so strong that ___ cannot cure.'
REVENGE	13. Iago's motive
GRATIANO	14. Brother of Brabantio
INNOCENT	15. Emilia said Desdemona was ___.
LOYALTY	16. Emilia's ___ to Iago proves stronger than her ___ to Desdemona.
REPUTATION	17. '___, ___, ___! Oh, I have lost my ___!'
OTHELLO	18. The jealous Moor
LIES	19. Iago told lots of these.
JEALOUSY	20. Motive for Othello's actions

Othello Matching 1

___ 1. REVENGE
___ 2. ACT
___ 3. LODOVICO
___ 4. PLAN
___ 5. LETTERS
___ 6. REPUTATION
___ 7. KNAVERY
___ 8. CASSIO
___ 9. NOSE
___10. DREAM
___11. BRABANTIO
___12. OTHELLO
___13. SHAKESPEARE
___14. EMILIA
___15. YEARS
___16. WORK
___17. CONFESSED
___18. DOG
___19. LIES
___20. WEB
___21. RODERIGO
___22. AM
___23. IAGO
___24. SCENE
___25. DIE

A. 'Oh, damned Iago! Oh, inhuman ___!'
B. '...you shall more command with ___ Than with your weapons.'
C. 'I ___ not what I ___.'
D. '___ on, My medicine, ___!'
E. Desdemona's father
F. Iago lied & told Othello Cassio had a ___ in which he cried out to Desdemona.
G. 'The Moor ... will as tenderly be led by the ___ As asses are.'
H. 'There's magic in the ___ of it.'
I. Plot; scheme
J. Author William
K. These, found in Roderigo's pockets, were evidence against Iago.
L. Act division
M. Tells of the letter found in Roderigo's pockets
N. 'Yet she must ___, else she'll betray more men.'
O. Play division
P. The jealous Moor
Q. Iago's motive
R. Becomes Lord Governor at the end of the play
S. Iago told lots of these.
T. Iago's actions ___ his guilt.
U. He is love-sick for Desdemona.
V. '...___'s plain face is never seen till used.'
W. Iago's wife; Desdemona's servant
X. '___, ___, ___! Oh, I have lost my ___!'
Y. He was passed over for promotion.

Othello Matching 1 Answer Key

Q - 1. REVENGE
O - 2. ACT
M - 3. LODOVICO
I - 4. PLAN
K - 5. LETTERS
X - 6. REPUTATION
V - 7. KNAVERY
R - 8. CASSIO
G - 9. NOSE
F - 10. DREAM
E - 11. BRABANTIO
P - 12. OTHELLO
J - 13. SHAKESPEARE
W - 14. EMILIA
B - 15. YEARS
D - 16. WORK
T - 17. CONFESSED
A - 18. DOG
S - 19. LIES
H - 20. WEB
U - 21. RODERIGO
C - 22. AM
Y - 23. IAGO
L - 24. SCENE
N - 25. DIE

A. 'Oh, damned Iago! Oh, inhuman ___!'
B. '...you shall more command with ___ Than with your weapons.'
C. 'I ___ not what I ___.'
D. '___ on, My medicine, ___!'
E. Desdemona's father
F. Iago lied & told Othello Cassio had a ___ in which he cried out to Desdemona.
G. 'The Moor ... will as tenderly be led by the ___ As asses are.'
H. 'There's magic in the ___ of it.'
I. Plot; scheme
J. Author William
K. These, found in Roderigo's pockets, were evidence against Iago.
L. Act division
M. Tells of the letter found in Roderigo's pockets
N. 'Yet she must ___, else she'll betray more men.'
O. Play division
P. The jealous Moor
Q. Iago's motive
R. Becomes Lord Governor at the end of the play
S. Iago told lots of these.
T. Iago's actions ___ his guilt.
U. He is love-sick for Desdemona.
V. '...___'s plain face is never seen till used.'
W. Iago's wife; Desdemona's servant
X. '___, ___, ___! Oh, I have lost my ___!'
Y. He was passed over for promotion.

Othello Matching 2

___ 1. SCENE
___ 2. IAGO
___ 3. RODERIGO
___ 4. BRABANTIO
___ 5. SHAKESPEARE
___ 6. KNAVERY
___ 7. SEEM
___ 8. HUSBAND
___ 9. REVENGE
___ 10. HANDKERCHIEF
___ 11. BIANCA
___ 12. DIE
___ 13. HATE
___ 14. EMILIA
___ 15. AM
___ 16. LOYALTY
___ 17. DREAM
___ 18. DESDEMONA
___ 19. GRATIANO
___ 20. LIES
___ 21. STABS
___ 22. CASSIO
___ 23. CONFESSED
___ 24. ACT
___ 25. NOBODY

A. Iago's wife; Desdemona's servant
B. 'I ___ not what I ___.'
C. '...___'s plain face is never seen till used.'
D. Becomes Lord Governor at the end of the play
E. Desdemona's father
F. 'Men should be what they ___.'
G. 'For naught did I in ___, but all in honor.'
H. Brother of Brabantio
I. Author William
J. Iago's actions ___ his guilt.
K. Iago lied & told Othello Cassio had a ___ in which he cried out to Desdemona.
L. Cassio's mistress
M. Act division
N. Othello to Desdemona
O. Iago told lots of these.
P. Emilia's ___ to Iago proves stronger than her ___ to Desdemona.
Q. Othello's wife
R. '___, I myself. Farewell.'
S. Play division
T. Personal item belonging to Desdemona; Othello thinks she gave it to Cassio
U. He is love-sick for Desdemona.
V. Othello ___ himself and dies.
W. Iago's motive
X. He was passed over for promotion.
Y. 'Yet she must ___, else she'll betray more men.'

Othello Matching 2 Answer Key

M - 1.	SCENE	A. Iago's wife; Desdemona's servant
X - 2.	IAGO	B. 'I ___ not what I ___.'
U - 3.	RODERIGO	C. '...___'s plain face is never seen till used.'
E - 4.	BRABANTIO	D. Becomes Lord Governor at the end of the play
I - 5.	SHAKESPEARE	E. Desdemona's father
C - 6.	KNAVERY	F. 'Men should be what they ___.'
F - 7.	SEEM	G. 'For naught did I in ___, but all in honor.'
N - 8.	HUSBAND	H. Brother of Brabantio
W - 9.	REVENGE	I. Author William
T - 10.	HANDKERCHIEF	J. Iago's actions ___ his guilt.
L - 11.	BIANCA	K. Iago lied & told Othello Cassio had a ___ in which he cried out to Desdemona.
Y - 12.	DIE	L. Cassio's mistress
G - 13.	HATE	M. Act division
A - 14.	EMILIA	N. Othello to Desdemona
B - 15.	AM	O. Iago told lots of these.
P - 16.	LOYALTY	P. Emilia's ___ to Iago proves stronger than her ___ to Desdemona.
K - 17.	DREAM	Q. Othello's wife
Q - 18.	DESDEMONA	R. '___, I myself. Farewell.'
H - 19.	GRATIANO	S. Play division
O - 20.	LIES	T. Personal item belonging to Desdemona; Othello thinks she gave it to Cassio
V - 21.	STABS	U. He is love-sick for Desdemona.
D - 22.	CASSIO	V. Othello ___ himself and dies.
J - 23.	CONFESSED	W. Iago's motive
S - 24.	ACT	X. He was passed over for promotion.
R - 25.	NOBODY	Y. 'Yet she must ___, else she'll betray more men.'

Copyrighted

Othello Matching 3

___ 1. FRIENDSHIP A. Iago's motive

___ 2. HATE B. Iago lied & told Othello Cassio had a ___ in which he cried out to Desdemona.

___ 3. DIE C. Iago told lots of these.

___ 4. VIRTUE D. '___, I myself. Farewell.'

___ 5. PLAN E. Act division

___ 6. NOBODY F. 'Yet she must ___, else she'll betray more men.'

___ 7. LIES G. The jealous Moor

___ 8. EMILIA H. Emilia said Desdemona was ___.

___ 9. AM I. Becomes Lord Governor at the end of the play

___ 10. DREAM J. Plot; scheme

___ 11. HUSBAND K. 'For naught did I in ___, but all in honor.'

___ 12. REVENGE L. 'I ___ not what I ___.'

___ 13. STABS M. Iago's wife; Desdemona's servant

___ 14. JUDGEMENT N. 'So I will turn her ___ into pitch....'

___ 15. REPUTATION O. These, found in Roderigo's pockets, were evidence against Iago.

___ 16. INNOCENT P. '...___'s plain face is never seen till used.'

___ 17. SEEM Q. Emilia's ___ to Iago proves stronger than her ___ to Desdemona.

___ 18. BIANCA R. 'Men should be what they ___.'

___ 19. WEB S. 'There's magic in the ___ of it.'

___ 20. LOYALTY T. '... yet that I put the Moor At least into a jealousy so strong that ___ cannot cure.'

___ 21. OTHELLO U. Othello ___ himself and dies.

___ 22. SCENE V. Othello to Desdemona

___ 23. KNAVERY W. Cassio's mistress

___ 24. LETTERS X. '___, ___, ___! Oh, I have lost my ___!'

___ 25. CASSIO Y. Othello's ___ with Iago keeps him from questioning Iago's loyalty.

Othello Matching 3 Answer Key

Y - 1. FRIENDSHIP	A.	Iago's motive
K - 2. HATE	B.	Iago lied & told Othello Cassio had a ___ in which he cried out to Desdemona.
F - 3. DIE	C.	Iago told lots of these.
N - 4. VIRTUE	D.	'___, I myself. Farewell.'
J - 5. PLAN	E.	Act division
D - 6. NOBODY	F.	'Yet she must ___, else she'll betray more men.'
C - 7. LIES	G.	The jealous Moor
M - 8. EMILIA	H.	Emilia said Desdemona was ___.
L - 9. AM	I.	Becomes Lord Governor at the end of the play
B -10. DREAM	J.	Plot; scheme
V -11. HUSBAND	K.	'For naught did I in ___, but all in honor.'
A -12. REVENGE	L.	'I ___ not what I ___.'
U -13. STABS	M.	Iago's wife; Desdemona's servant
T -14. JUDGEMENT	N.	'So I will turn her ___ into pitch....'
X -15. REPUTATION	O.	These, found in Roderigo's pockets, were evidence against Iago.
H -16. INNOCENT	P.	'...___'s plain face is never seen till used.'
R -17. SEEM	Q.	Emilia's ___ to Iago proves stronger than her ___ to Desdemona.
W -18. BIANCA	R.	'Men should be what they ___.'
S -19. WEB	S.	'There's magic in the ___ of it.'
Q -20. LOYALTY	T.	'... yet that I put the Moor At least into a jealousy so strong that ___ cannot cure.'
G -21. OTHELLO	U.	Othello ___ himself and dies.
E -22. SCENE	V.	Othello to Desdemona
P -23. KNAVERY	W.	Cassio's mistress
O -24. LETTERS	X.	'___, ___, ___! Oh, I have lost my ___!'
I -25. CASSIO	Y.	Othello's ___ with Iago keeps him from questioning Iago's loyalty.

Othello Matching 4

___ 1. BIANCA   A. Othello's ___ with Iago keeps him from questioning Iago's loyalty.
___ 2. WORK   B. 'So I will turn her ___ into pitch....'
___ 3. GRATIANO   C. Emilia's ___ to Iago proves stronger than her ___ to Desdemona.
___ 4. OTHELLO   D. 'I __ not what I __.'
___ 5. FRIENDSHIP   E. Othello ___ himself and dies.
___ 6. KNAVERY   F. Emilia to Iago
___ 7. STABS   G. 'Men should be what they ___.'
___ 8. ACT   H. Plot; scheme
___ 9. IAGO   I. Othello's heritage
___10. BRABANTIO   J. Personal item belonging to Desdemona; Othello thinks she gave it to Cassio
___11. SEEM   K. Motive for Othello's actions
___12. NET   L. '___ on, My medicine, ___!'
___13. HATE   M. 'For naught did I in ___, but all in honor.'
___14. REPUTATION   N. He is love-sick for Desdemona.
___15. WIFE   O. '...you shall more command with ___ Than with your weapons.'
___16. YEARS   P. Othello to Desdemona
___17. LOYALTY   Q. The jealous Moor
___18. PLAN   R. '___, ___, ___! Oh, I have lost my ___!'
___19. HANDKERCHIEF   S. Desdemona's father
___20. RODERIGO   T. Brother of Brabantio
___21. MOOR   U. Play division
___22. VIRTUE   V. 'And out of her own goodness make the ___ that shall enmesh them all.'
___23. JEALOUSY   W. '...___'s plain face is never seen till used.'
___24. HUSBAND   X. Cassio's mistress
___25. AM   Y. He was passed over for promotion.

Othello Matching 4 Answer Key

X - 1. BIANCA	A. Othello's ___ with Iago keeps him from questioning Iago's loyalty.
L - 2. WORK	B. 'So I will turn her ___ into pitch....'
T - 3. GRATIANO	C. Emilia's ___ to Iago proves stronger than her ___ to Desdemona.
Q - 4. OTHELLO	D. 'I ___ not what I ___.'
A - 5. FRIENDSHIP	E. Othello ___ himself and dies.
W - 6. KNAVERY	F. Emilia to Iago
E - 7. STABS	G. 'Men should be what they ___.'
U - 8. ACT	H. Plot; scheme
Y - 9. IAGO	I. Othello's heritage
S - 10. BRABANTIO	J. Personal item belonging to Desdemona; Othello thinks she gave it to Cassio
G - 11. SEEM	K. Motive for Othello's actions
V - 12. NET	L. '___ on, My medicine, ___!'
M - 13. HATE	M. 'For naught did I in ___, but all in honor.'
R - 14. REPUTATION	N. He is love-sick for Desdemona.
F - 15. WIFE	O. '...you shall more command with ___ Than with your weapons.'
O - 16. YEARS	P. Othello to Desdemona
C - 17. LOYALTY	Q. The jealous Moor
H - 18. PLAN	R. '___, ___, ___! Oh, I have lost my ___!'
J - 19. HANDKERCHIEF	S. Desdemona's father
N - 20. RODERIGO	T. Brother of Brabantio
I - 21. MOOR	U. Play division
B - 22. VIRTUE	V. 'And out of her own goodness make the ___ that shall enmesh them all.'
K - 23. JEALOUSY	W. '...___'s plain face is never seen till used.'
P - 24. HUSBAND	X. Cassio's mistress
D - 25. AM	Y. He was passed over for promotion.

Othello Magic Squares 1

Match the definition with the vocabulary word. Put your answers in the magic squares below. When your answers are correct, all columns and rows will add to the same number.

A. NOSE   E. WORK   I. HONESTY   M. NOBODY
B. SCENE   F. YEARS   J. VIRTUE   N. FRIENDSHIP
C. HANDKERCHIEF   G. CONFESSED   K. BRABANTIO   O. DIE
D. LOYALTY   H. ACT   L. REVENGE   P. HATE

1. '___, I myself. Farewell.'
2. '...you shall more command with ___ Than with your weapons.'
3. Play division
4. 'Yet she must ___, else she'll betray more men.'
5. Iago's motive
6. Personal item belonging to Desdemona; Othello thinks she gave it to Cassio
7. 'The Moor ... will as tenderly be led by the ___ As asses are.'
8. 'So I will turn her ___ into pitch....'
9. Desdemona's father
10. Emilia's ___ to Iago proves stronger than her ___ to Desdemona.
11. Act division
12. 'So please your Grace, my Ancient, a man he is of ___ and trust....'
13. Othello's ___ with Iago keeps him from questioning Iago's loyalty.
14. '___ on, My medicine, ___!'
15. Iago's actions ___ his guilt.
16. 'For naught did I in ___, but all in honor.'

A=	B=	C=	D=
E=	F=	G=	H=
I=	J=	K=	L=
M=	N=	O=	P=

Othello Magic Squares 1 Answer Key

Match the definition with the vocabulary word. Put your answers in the magic squares below. When your answers are correct, all columns and rows will add to the same number.

A. NOSE
B. SCENE
C. HANDKERCHIEF
D. LOYALTY
E. WORK
F. YEARS
G. CONFESSED
H. ACT
I. HONESTY
J. VIRTUE
K. BRABANTIO
L. REVENGE
M. NOBODY
N. FRIENDSHIP
O. DIE
P. HATE

1. '___, I myself. Farewell.'
2. '...you shall more command with ___ Than with your weapons.'
3. Play division
4. 'Yet she must ___, else she'll betray more men.'
5. Iago's motive
6. Personal item belonging to Desdemona; Othello thinks she gave it to Cassio
7. 'The Moor ... will as tenderly be led by the ___ As asses are.'
8. 'So I will turn her ___ into pitch....'
9. Desdemona's father
10. Emilia's ___ to Iago proves stronger than her ___ to Desdemona.
11. Act division
12. 'So please your Grace, my Ancient, a man he is of ___ and trust....'
13. Othello's ___ with Iago keeps him from questioning Iago's loyalty.
14. '___ on, My medicine, ___!'
15. Iago's actions ___ his guilt.
16. 'For naught did I in ___, but all in honor.'

A=7	B=11	C=6	D=10
E=14	F=2	G=15	H=3
I=12	J=8	K=9	L=5
M=1	N=13	O=4	P=16

Othello Magic Squares 2

Match the definition with the vocabulary word. Put your answers in the magic squares below. When your answers are correct, all columns and rows will add to the same number.

A. PLAN
B. WIFE
C. LIES
D. SCENE
E. KNAVERY
F. WORK
G. SHAKESPEARE
H. LOYALTY
I. ACT
J. DREAM
K. LETTERS
L. RODERIGO
M. YEARS
N. DIE
O. CONFESSED
P. IAGO

1. Emilia's ___ to Iago proves stronger than her ___ to Desdemona.
2. Plot; scheme
3. Emilia to Iago
4. Author William
5. Iago lied & told Othello Cassio had a ___ in which he cried out to Desdemona.
6. Iago's actions ___ his guilt.
7. He was passed over for promotion.
8. Play division
9. These, found in Roderigo's pockets, were evidence against Iago.
10. 'Yet she must ___, else she'll betray more men.'
11. '...you shall more command with ___ Than with your weapons.'
12. He is love-sick for Desdemona.
13. '...___'s plain face is never seen till used.'
14. Act division
15. Iago told lots of these.
16. '___ on, My medicine, ___!'

A=	B=	C=	D=
E=	F=	G=	H=
I=	J=	K=	L=
M=	N=	O=	P=

Othello Magic Squares 2 Answer Key

Match the definition with the vocabulary word. Put your answers in the magic squares below. When your answers are correct, all columns and rows will add to the same number.

A. PLAN
B. WIFE
C. LIES
D. SCENE
E. KNAVERY
F. WORK
G. SHAKESPEARE
H. LOYALTY
I. ACT
J. DREAM
K. LETTERS
L. RODERIGO
M. YEARS
N. DIE
O. CONFESSED
P. IAGO

1. Emilia's ___ to Iago proves stronger than her ___ to Desdemona.
2. Plot; scheme
3. Emilia to Iago
4. Author William
5. Iago lied & told Othello Cassio had a ___ in which he cried out to Desdemona.
6. Iago's actions ___ his guilt.
7. He was passed over for promotion.
8. Play division
9. These, found in Roderigo's pockets, were evidence against Iago.
10. 'Yet she must ___, else she'll betray more men.'
11. '...you shall more command with ___ Than with your weapons.'
12. He is love-sick for Desdemona.
13. '...___'s plain face is never seen till used.'
14. Act division
15. Iago told lots of these.
16. '___ on, My medicine, ___!'

A=2	B=3	C=15	D=14
E=13	F=16	G=4	H=1
I=8	J=5	K=9	L=12
M=11	N=10	O=6	P=7

24
Copyrighted

Othello Magic Squares 3

Match the definition with the vocabulary word. Put your answers in the magic squares below. When your answers are correct, all columns and rows will add to the same number.

A. LIES	E. KNAVERY	I. REPUTATION	M. DIE
B. DREAM	F. VIRTUE	J. YEARS	N. INNOCENT
C. LETTERS	G. PLAN	K. OTHELLO	O. LODOVICO
D. ACT	H. NET	L. DESDEMONA	P. CASSIO

1. 'And out of her own goodness make the ___ that shall enmesh them all.'
2. 'Yet she must ___, else she'll betray more men.'
3. Iago lied & told Othello Cassio had a ___ in which he cried out to Desdemona.
4. The jealous Moor
5. '...you shall more command with ___ Than with your weapons.'
6. These, found in Roderigo's pockets, were evidence against Iago.
7. Becomes Lord Governor at the end of the play
8. '...___'s plain face is never seen till used.'
9. Tells of the letter found in Roderigo's pockets
10. 'So I will turn her ___ into pitch....'
11. '___, ___, ___! Oh, I have lost my ___!'
12. Play division
13. Iago told lots of these.
14. Othello's wife
15. Plot; scheme
16. Emilia said Desdemona was ___.

A=	B=	C=	D=
E=	F=	G=	H=
I=	J=	K=	L=
M=	N=	O=	P=

Othello Magic Squares 3 Answer Key

Match the definition with the vocabulary word. Put your answers in the magic squares below. When your answers are correct, all columns and rows will add to the same number.

A. LIES
B. DREAM
C. LETTERS
D. ACT
E. KNAVERY
F. VIRTUE
G. PLAN
H. NET
I. REPUTATION
J. YEARS
K. OTHELLO
L. DESDEMONA
M. DIE
N. INNOCENT
O. LODOVICO
P. CASSIO

1. 'And out of her own goodness make the ___ that shall enmesh them all.'
2. 'Yet she must ___, else she'll betray more men.'
3. Iago lied & told Othello Cassio had a ___ in which he cried out to Desdemona.
4. The jealous Moor
5. '...you shall more command with ___ Than with your weapons.'
6. These, found in Roderigo's pockets, were evidence against Iago.
7. Becomes Lord Governor at the end of the play
8. '...___'s plain face is never seen till used.'
9. Tells of the letter found in Roderigo's pockets
10. 'So I will turn her ___ into pitch....'
11. '___, ___, ___! Oh, I have lost my ___!'
12. Play division
13. Iago told lots of these.
14. Othello's wife
15. Plot; scheme
16. Emilia said Desdemona was ___.

A=13	B=3	C=6	D=12
E=8	F=10	G=15	H=1
I=11	J=5	K=4	L=14
M=2	N=16	O=9	P=7

Othello Magic Squares 4

Match the definition with the vocabulary word. Put your answers in the magic squares below. When your answers are correct, all columns and rows will add to the same number.

A. CONFESSED   E. JEALOUSY   I. STABS   M. HUSBAND
B. SEEM   F. KNAVERY   J. DREAM   N. INNOCENT
C. EMILIA   G. DESDEMONA   K. SCENE   O. YEARS
D. LETTERS   H. ACT   L. AM   P. DOG

1. 'Men should be what they ___.'
2. Othello's wife
3. Act division
4. Emilia said Desdemona was ___.
5. Othello to Desdemona
6. 'I __ not what I __.'
7. Play division
8. Iago's actions ___ his guilt.
9. 'Oh, damned Iago! Oh, inhuman __!'
10. Othello ___ himself and dies.
11. Motive for Othello's actions
12. These, found in Roderigo's pockets, were evidence against Iago.
13. Iago's wife; Desdemona's servant
14. '...___'s plain face is never seen till used.'
15. Iago lied & told Othello Cassio had a ___ in which he cried out to Desdemona.
16. '...you shall more command with ___ Than with your weapons.'

A=	B=	C=	D=
E=	F=	G=	H=
I=	J=	K=	L=
M=	N=	O=	P=

Othello Magic Squares 4 Answer Key

Match the definition with the vocabulary word. Put your answers in the magic squares below. When your answers are correct, all columns and rows will add to the same number.

A. CONFESSED   E. JEALOUSY   I. STABS   M. HUSBAND
B. SEEM   F. KNAVERY   J. DREAM   N. INNOCENT
C. EMILIA   G. DESDEMONA   K. SCENE   O. YEARS
D. LETTERS   H. ACT   L. AM   P. DOG

1. 'Men should be what they ___.'
2. Othello's wife
3. Act division
4. Emilia said Desdemona was ___.
5. Othello to Desdemona
6. 'I ___ not what I ___.'
7. Play division
8. Iago's actions ___ his guilt.
9. 'Oh, damned Iago! Oh, inhuman ___!'
10. Othello ___ himself and dies.
11. Motive for Othello's actions
12. These, found in Roderigo's pockets, were evidence against Iago.
13. Iago's wife; Desdemona's servant
14. '...___'s plain face is never seen till used.'
15. Iago lied & told Othello Cassio had a ___ in which he cried out to Desdemona.
16. '...you shall more command with ___ Than with your weapons.'

A=8	B=1	C=13	D=12
A=11	F=14	G=2	H=7
I=10	J=15	K=3	L=6
M=5	N=4	O=16	P=9

Othello Word Search 1

```
R J H S C N S C H S L B M V I R T U E
O U U K A W T P A X O R U F J T X N R
D D S S S Z A J N B D A R J W S V W A
E G B W S V B N D Z O B D M S S X B E
R E A F I B S R K M V A E M I L I A P
I M N C O F C L E S I N R R R F W X S
G E D V P C E D R H C T M E J Q T N E
O N S C E N E K C W O I R V L K N O K
T T N J Y R F N H M V O N E E V E I A
K V H O X B X A I P P S M N T D C T H
P T G O B C Z V E F R P S G T H O A S
B Z G W N O K E F A D D N E E F N T D
Z I R R M E D R E L N R P O R K N U E
J E A L O U S Y F R I E N D S H I P S
D C T N D T T T Q B T A T E M E L E D
T T I M C L H L Y A B M I M P A E R E
A C A P A A B E H T W L I K N D F M M
L M N Y W E B N L M O O R A S O S M O
J G O Z I H Z D K L H Y R V G G K Q N
S L V D E S S E F N O C M K F O X C A
```

'... yet that I put the Moor At least into a jealousy so strong that ___ cannot cure.' (9)
'...___'s plain face is never seen till used.' (7)
'...you shall more command with ___ Than with your weapons.' (5)
'And out of her own goodness make the ___ that shall enmesh them all.' (3)
'For naught did I in ___, but all in honor.' (4)
'I ___ not what I ___.' (2)
'Men should be what they ___.' (4)
'Oh, damned Iago! Oh, inhuman ___!' (3)
'So I will turn her ___ into pitch....' (6)
'So please your Grace, my Ancient, a man he is of ___ and trust....' (7)
'The Moor ... will as tenderly be led by the ___ As asses are.' (4)
'There's magic in the ___ of it.' (3)
'Yet she must ___, else she'll betray more men.' (3)
'___ on, My medicine, ___!' (4)
'___, I myself. Farewell.' (6)
'___, ___, ___! Oh, I have lost my ___!' (10)
Act division (5)
Author William (11)
Becomes Lord Governor at the end of the play (6)
Brother of Brabantio (8)
Cassio's mistress (6)
Desdemona's father (9)
Emilia said Desdemona was ___. (8)
Emilia to Iago (4)
Emilia's ___ to Iago proves stronger than her ___ to Desdemona. (7)
He is love-sick for Desdemona. (8)
He was passed over for promotion. (4)
Iago lied & told Othello Cassio had a ___ in which he cried out to Desdemona. (5)
Iago plots to ___ Cassio (6)
Iago told lots of these. (4)
Iago's actions ___ his guilt. (9)
Iago's motive (7)
Iago's wife; Desdemona's servant (6)
Motive for Othello's actions (8)
Othello ___ himself and dies. (5)
Othello to Desdemona (7)
Othello's ___ with Iago keeps him from questioning Iago's loyalty. (10)
Othello's heritage (4)
Othello's wife (9)
Personal item belonging to Desdemona; Othello thinks she gave it to Cassio (12)
Play division (3)
Plot; scheme (4)
Tells of the letter found in Roderigo's pockets (8)
The jealous Moor (7)
These, found in Roderigo's pockets, were evidence against Iago. (7)

Othello Word Search 1 Answer Key

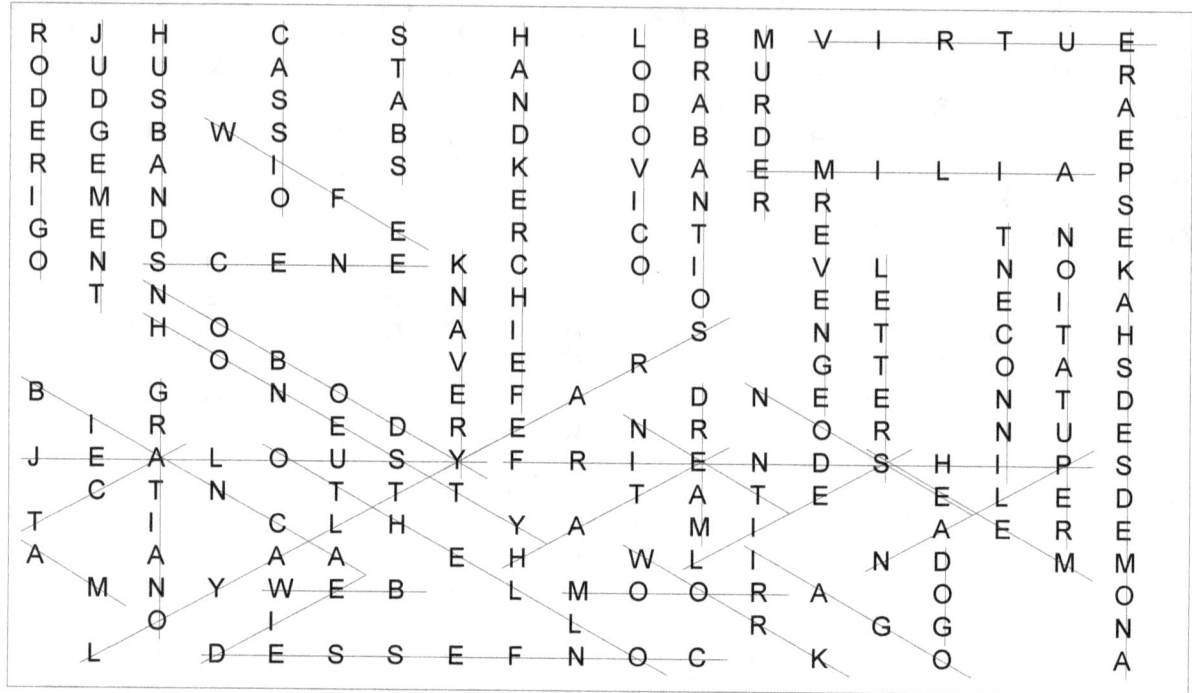

'... yet that I put the Moor At least into a jealousy so strong that ___ cannot cure.' (9)
'...___'s plain face is never seen till used.' (7)
'...you shall more command with ___ Than with your weapons.' (5)
'And out of her own goodness make the ___ that shall enmesh them all.' (3)
'For naught did I in ___, but all in honor.' (4)
'I ___ not what I ___.' (2)
'Men should be what they ___.' (4)
'Oh, damned Iago! Oh, inhuman ___!' (3)
'So I will turn her ___ into pitch....' (6)
'So please your Grace, my Ancient, a man he is of ___ and trust....' (7)
'The Moor ... will as tenderly be led by the ___ As asses are.' (4)
'There's magic in the ___ of it.' (3)
'Yet she must ___, else she'll betray more men.' (3)
'___ on, My medicine, ___!' (4)
'___, I myself. Farewell.' (6)
'___, ___, ___! Oh, I have lost my ___!' (10)
Act division (5)
Author William (11)
Becomes Lord Governor at the end of the play (6)
Brother of Brabantio (8)
Cassio's mistress (6)
Desdemona's father (9)
Emilia said Desdemona was ___. (8)
Emilia to Iago (4)
Emilia's ___ to Iago proves stronger than her ___ to Desdemona. (7)
He is love-sick for Desdemona. (8)
He was passed over for promotion. (4)
Iago lied & told Othello Cassio had a ___ in which he cried out to Desdemona. (5)
Iago plots to ___ Cassio (6)
Iago told lots of these. (4)
Iago's actions ___ his guilt. (9)
Iago's motive (7)
Iago's wife; Desdemona's servant (6)
Motive for Othello's actions (8)
Othello ___ himself and dies. (5)
Othello to Desdemona (7)
Othello's ___ with Iago keeps him from questioning Iago's loyalty. (10)
Othello's heritage (4)
Othello's wife (9)
Personal item belonging to Desdemona; Othello thinks she gave it to Cassio (12)
Play division (3)
Plot; scheme (4)
Tells of the letter found in Roderigo's pockets (8)
The jealous Moor (7)
These, found in Roderigo's pockets, were evidence against Iago. (7)

Othello Word Search 2

```
G R A T I A N O R T C M J L X N X R F
V Y T C G X I K N O U O O C F D S E E
K S N L K S C Y D R D Y N O R F H V I
Q C N B S H W S D F A E E F R G B E H
X J K A K U B E J L N L R M E Y K N C
B L C X F S R D T S F Q A I X S T G R
P D D J X B A Y J R R H E B G Z S E E
E M I L I A B H U W I O P K N O A E K
J K F X V N A H D C E C S I W R N G D
P S N C H D N O G N N I E N F X O P N
L C N A D W T N E O D V K N Z H M C A
C X O W V Z I E M B S O A O L Q E M H
S Y I V J E O S E O H D H C D A D H V
P S T Z J D R T N D I O S E C R S B A
J E A L O U S Y T Y P L A N S E E M X
X K T R C W E S W I N D A T E W D A G
M Y U X I A T C O A G I A N I T S X M
W W P F R M A E R G B B F J L H R D D
D I E S O N H N K O S O T H E L L O H
V I R T U E L E T T E R S A C T K G L
```

'... yet that I put the Moor At least into a jealousy so strong that ___ cannot cure.' (9)
'...___'s plain face is never seen till used.' (7)
'...you shall more command with ___ Than with your weapons.' (5)
'And out of her own goodness make the ___ that shall enmesh them all.' (3)
'For naught did I in ___, but all in honor.' (4)
'I __ not what I __.' (2)
'Men should be what they ___.' (4)
'Oh, damned Iago! Oh, inhuman __!' (3)
'So I will turn her ___ into pitch....' (6)
'So please your Grace, my Ancient, a man he is of ___ and trust....' (7)
'The Moor ... will as tenderly be led by the ___ As asses are.' (4)
'There's magic in the ___ of it.' (3)
'Yet she must ___, else she'll betray more men.' (3)
'___ on, My medicine, ___!' (4)
'___, I myself. Farewell.' (6)
'___, ___, ___! Oh, I have lost my ___!' (10)
Act division (5)
Author William (11)
Becomes Lord Governor at the end of the play (6)
Brother of Brabantio (8)
Cassio's mistress (6)
Desdemona's father (9)
Emilia said Desdemona was ___. (8)
Emilia to Iago (4)
Emilia's ___ to Iago proves stronger than her ___ to Desdemona. (7)
He is love-sick for Desdemona. (8)
He was passed over for promotion. (4)
Iago lied & told Othello Cassio had a ___ in which he cried out to Desdemona. (5)
Iago plots to ___ Cassio (6)
Iago told lots of these. (4)
Iago's actions ___ his guilt. (9)
Iago's motive (7)
Iago's wife; Desdemona's servant (6)
Motive for Othello's actions (8)
Othello ___ himself and dies. (5)
Othello to Desdemona (7)
Othello's ___ with Iago keeps him from questioning Iago's loyalty. (10)
Othello's heritage (4)
Othello's wife (9)
Personal item belonging to Desdemona; Othello thinks she gave it to Cassio (12)
Play division (3)
Plot; scheme (4)
Tells of the letter found in Roderigo's pockets (8)
The jealous Moor (7)
These, found in Roderigo's pockets, were evidence against Iago. (7)

Othello Word Search 2 Answer Key

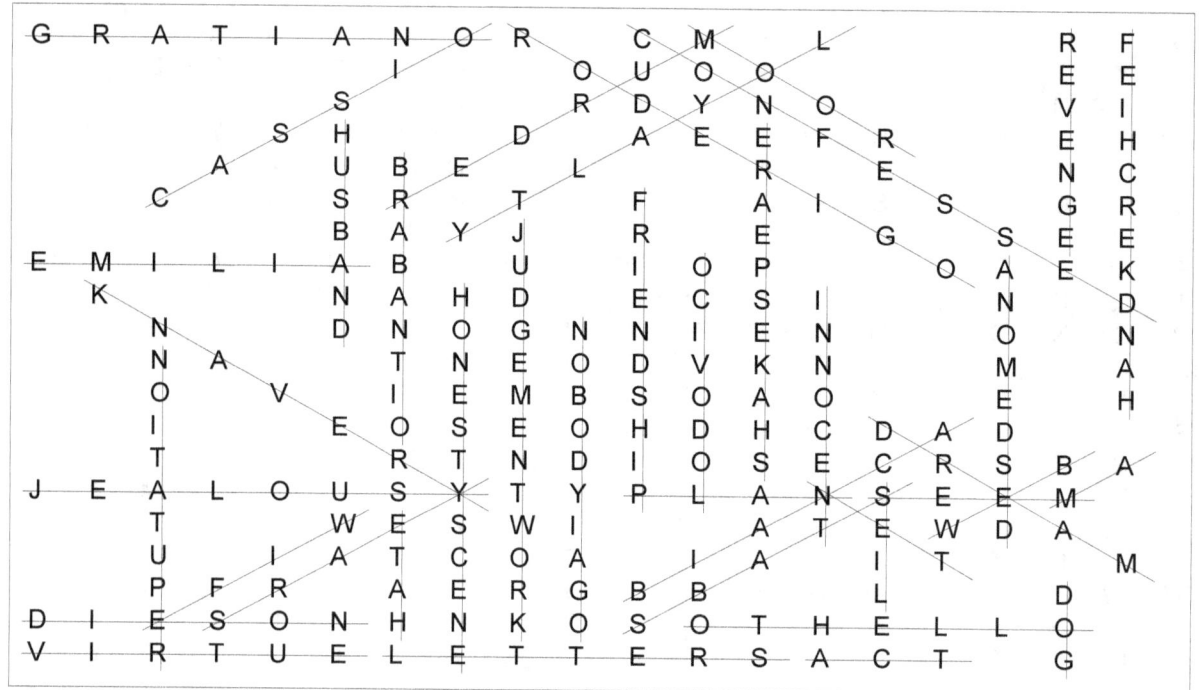

'... yet that I put the Moor At least into a jealousy so strong that ___ cannot cure.' (9)
'...___'s plain face is never seen till used.' (7)
'...you shall more command with ___ Than with your weapons.' (5)
'And out of her own goodness make the ___ that shall enmesh them all.' (3)
'For naught did I in ___, but all in honor.' (4)
'I __ not what I __.' (2)
'Men should be what they ___.' (4)
'Oh, damned Iago! Oh, inhuman __!' (3)
'So I will turn her ___ into pitch....' (6)
'So please your Grace, my Ancient, a man he is of ___ and trust....' (7)
'The Moor ... will as tenderly be led by the ___ As asses are.' (4)
'There's magic in the ___ of it.' (3)
'Yet she must ___, else she'll betray more men.' (3)
'___ on, My medicine, ___!' (4)
'___, I myself. Farewell.' (6)
'___, ___, ___! Oh, I have lost my ___!' (10)
Act division (5)
Author William (11)
Becomes Lord Governor at the end of the play (6)
Brother of Brabantio (8)
Cassio's mistress (6)
Desdemona's father (9)

Emilia said Desdemona was ___. (8)
Emilia to Iago (4)
Emilia's ___ to Iago proves stronger than her ___ to Desdemona. (7)
He is love-sick for Desdemona. (8)
He was passed over for promotion. (4)
Iago lied & told Othello Cassio had a ___ in which he cried out to Desdemona. (5)
Iago plots to ___ Cassio (6)
Iago told lots of these. (4)
Iago's actions ___ his guilt. (9)
Iago's motive (7)
Iago's wife; Desdemona's servant (6)
Motive for Othello's actions (8)
Othello ___ himself and dies. (5)
Othello to Desdemona (7)
Othello's ___ with Iago keeps him from questioning Iago's loyalty. (10)
Othello's heritage (4)
Othello's wife (9)
Personal item belonging to Desdemona; Othello thinks she gave it to Cassio (12)
Play division (3)
Plot; scheme (4)
Tells of the letter found in Roderigo's pockets (8)
The jealous Moor (7)
These, found in Roderigo's pockets, were evidence against Iago. (7)

Othello Word Search 3

```
J R X S M W N M Y Y Y K I F N C F R J
E R A E P S E K A H S R A E Y K R O W
A R E S M I C B J E A C G I T B I B
L S K O D I L E I S N C O H S R E D N
O P R N Q O L L N A N E T C E A N S D
U G L O Y T Y I I N D D R N B D A C N F
S R N A D H K B A M O O E E O A S C N M
Y A L E N E T A H O I G S K H N H A M
C T F F Q L R Z C O T B D D K T I M D
Y I J B S L E I F R A D E N N I P J J
W A X D L O V W G T T R M A A O H U K
F N N L H O E R S O E M O H V R D D D
D O K O D N N M X C P A N Q E I S G Q
K J W O B J G H G L E M A D R N B E W
V W L N W O E G K B R N R X Y N A M R
R I D N W Q D V Z X S U S B L O N E L
J F R M J S J Y F F M F Q Y S C D N G
P K R T B H D B W T J Q T L T E H T W
S Z Y J U L E T T E R S Q G X N M Q L
P C O N F E S S E D H D K V W T W Y N
```

ACT	GRATIANO	LODOVICO	SCENE
AM	HANDKERCHIEF	LOYALTY	SEEM
BIANCA	HATE	MOOR	SHAKESPEARE
BRABANTIO	HONESTY	MURDER	STABS
CASSIO	HUSBAND	NET	VIRTUE
CONFESSED	IAGO	NOBODY	WEB
DESDEMONA	INNOCENT	NOSE	WIFE
DIE	JEALOUSY	OTHELLO	WORK
DOG	JUDGEMENT	PLAN	YEARS
DREAM	KNAVERY	REPUTATION	
EMILIA	LETTERS	REVENGE	
FRIENDSHIP	LIES	RODERIGO	

Othello Word Search 3 Answer Key

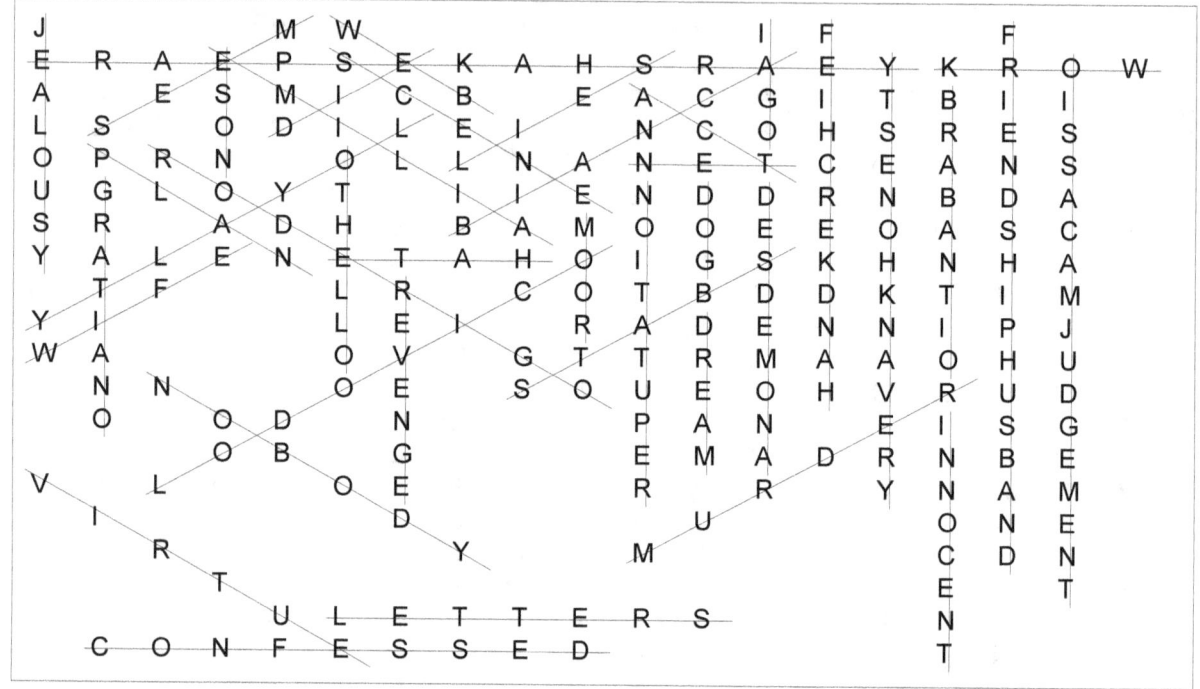

ACT	GRATIANO	LODOVICO	SCENE
AM	HANDKERCHIEF	LOYALTY	SEEM
BIANCA	HATE	MOOR	SHAKESPEARE
BRABANTIO	HONESTY	MURDER	STABS
CASSIO	HUSBAND	NET	VIRTUE
CONFESSED	IAGO	NOBODY	WEB
DESDEMONA	INNOCENT	NOSE	WIFE
DIE	JEALOUSY	OTHELLO	WORK
DOG	JUDGEMENT	PLAN	YEARS
DREAM	KNAVERY	REPUTATION	
EMILIA	LETTERS	REVENGE	
FRIENDSHIP	LIES	RODERIGO	

Othello Word Search 4

```
A M H U S B A N D O W E M I L I A L L
R K X N W R D L I T B O U I V W M O O
R K N T Z A H S S H I T R D A E K D Y
S O R B T B S R J E A H D K E G R O A
S Z D R Z A D I E L N K E S C Y O V L
F X R E C N P E N L C M R E C S V I T
K G E L R T W F S O A S T I D E J C Y
J J A W D I Z I V D D L T L H J N O D
B U M Y P O G B F E E T C A W E B E R
C S D F W R G O S E S M T S B K D G Y
Z Y N G R R J O P U S E O Q M S Q G H
G L O V E I N Q R T E I N N O C E N T
W J B S S M E Q G R F K A E A M J F N
G C O V H G E N W I N V I K T V E M V
P R D M O O R N D V O R T N R P A C W
X W Y B N N D M T S C C A A V T L T S
R E R A E P S E K A H S R V B J O A G
Y E A R S R E T T E L I G E N X U F G
R E P U T A T I O N Y S P R W W S X G
S Z W P Y N R E V E N G E Y G P Y F K
```

ACT	DREAM	JEALOUSY	NET	SEEM
AM	EMILIA	JUDGEMENT	NOBODY	SHAKESPEARE
BIANCA	FRIENDSHIP	KNAVERY	NOSE	STABS
BRABANTIO	GRATIANO	LETTERS	OTHELLO	VIRTUE
CASSIO	HATE	LIES	PLAN	WEB
CONFESSED	HONESTY	LODOVICO	REPUTATION	WIFE
DESDEMONA	HUSBAND	LOYALTY	REVENGE	WORK
DIE	IAGO	MOOR	RODERIGO	YEARS
DOG	INNOCENT	MURDER	SCENE	

Othello Word Search 4 Answer Key

```
A  M  H  U  S  B  A  N  D  O     W  E  M  I  L  I  A     L
         R           I     T  B  O  U     I     M  L  O  Y
   R     A        S     H  I        R     A  E     O  A
      O  B     D  E     E  A        D  K  E  G        D  L
         D  E  C     E     L  L     E  S  C        V  T
      R     N     T  W     L  O  D  R     E  I  H     I  Y
   J     D     I     G     O  F  E     S  T  L  H     C
      U  M     O     G  S  E  E  S  T  C  A  W  B  O  E
         D  F        G     O  U  S  M  T     B  S
         N  G  R  I  N        T  E  N  O  N  O  C  E  N  T
         O     E  M     N     R  I     A  E  A     J
         B     H           D  I  O  C  I  K  T  P  E
         D  M  O  O  R  N  D  V  S     T  N  A     A
         Y     N              T  C     A  V     L  L
      E     A  P  S  E  K  A  H  S  R  V  E  R  O  E
   Y  E  A  R  S  R  E  T  T  E  L     I  G     U  A     N
   R  E  P  U  T  A  T  I  O  N              P     S  Y
                     R  E  V  E  N  G  E  Y      Y
```

ACT	DREAM	JEALOUSY	NET	SEEM
AM	EMILIA	JUDGEMENT	NOBODY	SHAKESPEARE
BIANCA	FRIENDSHIP	KNAVERY	NOSE	STABS
BRABANTIO	GRATIANO	LETTERS	OTHELLO	VIRTUE
CASSIO	HATE	LIES	PLAN	WEB
CONFESSED	HONESTY	LODOVICO	REPUTATION	WIFE
DESDEMONA	HUSBAND	LOYALTY	REVENGE	WORK
DIE	IAGO	MOOR	RODERIGO	YEARS
DOG	INNOCENT	MURDER	SCENE	

Othello Crossword 1

Across

1. 'So please your Grace, my Ancient, a man he is of ___ and trust....'
5. Iago's wife; Desdemona's servant
7. 'The Moor ... will as tenderly be led by the ___ As asses are.'
9. '___, I myself. Farewell.'
12. 'Men should be what they ___.'
14. Play division
15. 'There's magic in the ___ of it.'
17. Tells of the letter found in Roderigo's pockets
19. Plot; scheme
22. 'I __ not what I __.'
23. 'And out of her own goodness make the ___ that shall enmesh them all.'
24. Emilia said Desdemona was ___.
25. These, found in Roderigo's pockets, were evidence against Iago.
26. Iago lied & told Othello Cassio had a ___ in which he cried out to Desdemona.
27. 'For naught did I in ___, but all in honor.'

Down

1. Personal item belonging to Desdemona; Othello thinks she gave it to Cassio
2. '...you shall more command with ___ Than with your weapons.'
3. Iago told lots of these.
4. Emilia to Iago
6. 'Oh, damned Iago! Oh, inhuman __!'
8. Author William
10. 'Yet she must ___, else she'll betray more men.'
11. The jealous Moor
13. Othello's heritage
15. '___ on, My medicine, ___!'
16. Desdemona's father
17. Emilia's ___ to Iago proves stronger than her ___ to Desdemona.
18. He was passed over for promotion.
20. 'So I will turn her ___ into pitch....'
21. Act division

Othello Crossword 1 Answer Key

	1 H	O	N	E	S	T	2 Y		3 L		4 W				
	A						5 E	M	I	L	I	A		6 D	
7 N	O	8 S	E			A		E		F		9 N	O	B	O	10 Y
	D		H		11 O		R		12 S	E	E	13 M		G		I	
	K		14 A	C	T		S				O			15 W	E	16 B
	E		K		H			17 L	O	D	O	V	18 I	C	O
	R		E		E			O		R		A		R	A
	C		S		L			Y				G		K		B
	H		P		L	19 P	L	A	N			O				A
	I		E		O			L		20 V		21 S		
	E	22 A	M	23 N	E	T		24 I	N	N	O	C	E	N	T
	F	R		Y			R			E		I
	25 L	E	T	T	E	R	S		T		N		O
								26 U		D	R	E	A	M
					27 H	A	T	E

Across
1. 'So please your Grace, my Ancient, a man he is of ___ and trust....'
5. Iago's wife; Desdemona's servant
7. 'The Moor ... will as tenderly be led by the ___ As asses are.'
9. '___, I myself. Farewell.'
12. 'Men should be what they ___.'
14. Play division
15. 'There's magic in the ___ of it.'
17. Tells of the letter found in Roderigo's pockets
19. Plot; scheme
22. 'I __ not what I __.'
23. 'And out of her own goodness make the ___ that shall enmesh them all.'
24. Emilia said Desdemona was ___.
25. These, found in Roderigo's pockets, were evidence against Iago.
26. Iago lied & told Othello Cassio had a ___ in which he cried out to Desdemona.
27. 'For naught did I in ___, but all in honor.'

Down
1. Personal item belonging to Desdemona; Othello thinks she gave it to Cassio
2. '...you shall more command with ___ Than with your weapons.'
3. Iago told lots of these.
4. Emilia to Iago
6. 'Oh, damned Iago! Oh, inhuman __!'
8. Author William
10. 'Yet she must ___, else she'll betray more men.'
11. The jealous Moor
13. Othello's heritage
15. '___ on, My medicine, ___!'
16. Desdemona's father
17. Emilia's ___ to Iago proves stronger than her ___ to Desdemona.
18. He was passed over for promotion.
20. 'So I will turn her ___ into pitch....'
21. Act division

Othello Crossword 2

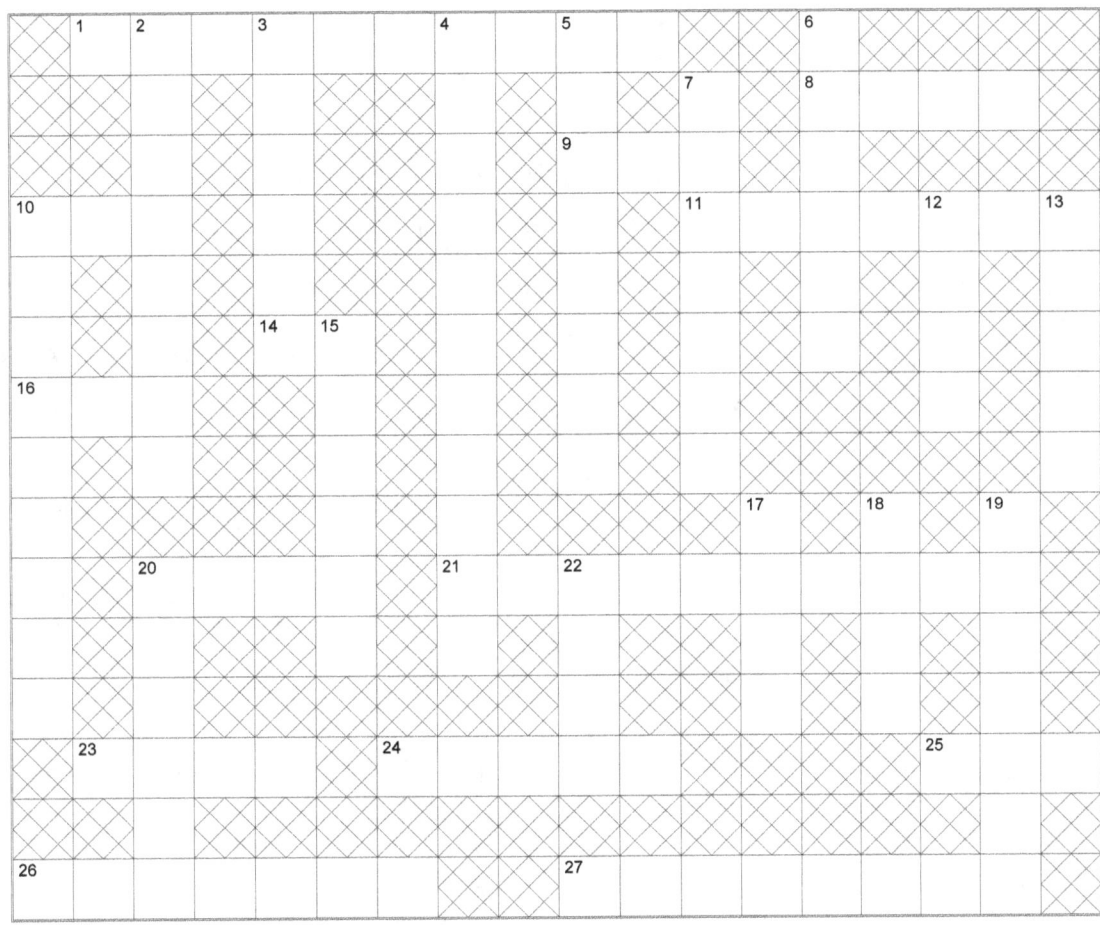

Across
1. Othello's ___ with Iago keeps him from questioning Iago's loyalty.
8. He was passed over for promotion.
9. 'And out of her own goodness make the ___ that shall enmesh them all.'
10. 'Yet she must ___, else she'll betray more men.'
11. 'So please your Grace, my Ancient, a man he is of ___ and trust....'
14. 'I ___ not what I ___.'
16. 'Oh, damned Iago! Oh, inhuman ___!'
20. 'The Moor ... will as tenderly be led by the ___ As asses are.'
21. '___, ___, ___! Oh, I have lost my ___!'
23. '___ on, My medicine, ___!'
24. Act division
25. 'There's magic in the ___ of it.'
26. Emilia's ___ to Iago proves stronger than her ___ to Desdemona.
27. Motive for Othello's actions

Down
2. He is love-sick for Desdemona.
3. Iago's wife; Desdemona's servant
4. Author William
5. Emilia said Desdemona was ___.
6. Cassio's mistress
7. The jealous Moor
10. Othello's wife
12. 'Men should be what they ___.'
13. '...you shall more command with ___ Than with your weapons.'
15. Iago plots to ___ Cassio
17. 'For naught did I in ___, but all in honor.'
18. Iago told lots of these.
19. '...___'s plain face is never seen till used.'
20. '___, I myself. Farewell.'
22. Plot; scheme

39
Copyrighted

Othello Crossword 2 Answer Key

	1 F	2 R	3 I	E	4 N	D	5 S	H	I	P	6 B		
		O		M			H		N	7 O	8 I	A	G	O
		D		I			A		9 N	E	T	A		
10 D	I	E		L			K		O	11 H	O	N	12 E	13 S	T	Y
E		R		I			E		C	E		C		E			E
S			14 I	15 A	M		S		E		L		A		E			A
16 D	O	G		U			P		N		L			M			R
E			O		R		E		T		O						S
M					D		A			17 H		18 L		19 K			
O		20 N	O	S	E		21 R	E	22 P	U	T	A	T	I	O	N
N		O			R			E		L		T		E			A
A		B						A				E		S		25		V
		23 W	O	R	K		24 S	C	E	N	E					W	E	B
				D												R		
26 L	O	Y	A	L	T	Y		27 J	E	A	L	O	U	S	Y		

Across
1. Othello's ___ with Iago keeps him from questioning Iago's loyalty.
8. He was passed over for promotion.
9. 'And out of her own goodness make the ___ that shall enmesh them all.'
10. 'Yet she must ___, else she'll betray more men.'
11. 'So please your Grace, my Ancient, a man he is of ___ and trust....'
14. 'I ___ not what I ___.'
16. 'Oh, damned Iago! Oh, inhuman ___!'
20. 'The Moor ... will as tenderly be led by the ___ As asses are.'
21. '___, ___, ___! Oh, I have lost my ___!'
23. '___ on, My medicine, ___!'
24. Act division
25. 'There's magic in the ___ of it.'
26. Emilia's ___ to Iago proves stronger than her ___ to Desdemona.
27. Motive for Othello's actions

Down
2. He is love-sick for Desdemona.
3. Iago's wife; Desdemona's servant
4. Author William
5. Emilia said Desdemona was ___.
6. Cassio's mistress
7. The jealous Moor
10. Othello's wife
12. 'Men should be what they ___.'
13. '...you shall more command with ___ Than with your weapons.'
15. Iago plots to ___ Cassio
17. 'For naught did I in ___, but all in honor.'
18. Iago told lots of these.
19. '___'s plain face is never seen till used.'
20. '___, I myself. Farewell.'
22. Plot; scheme

Othello Crossword 3

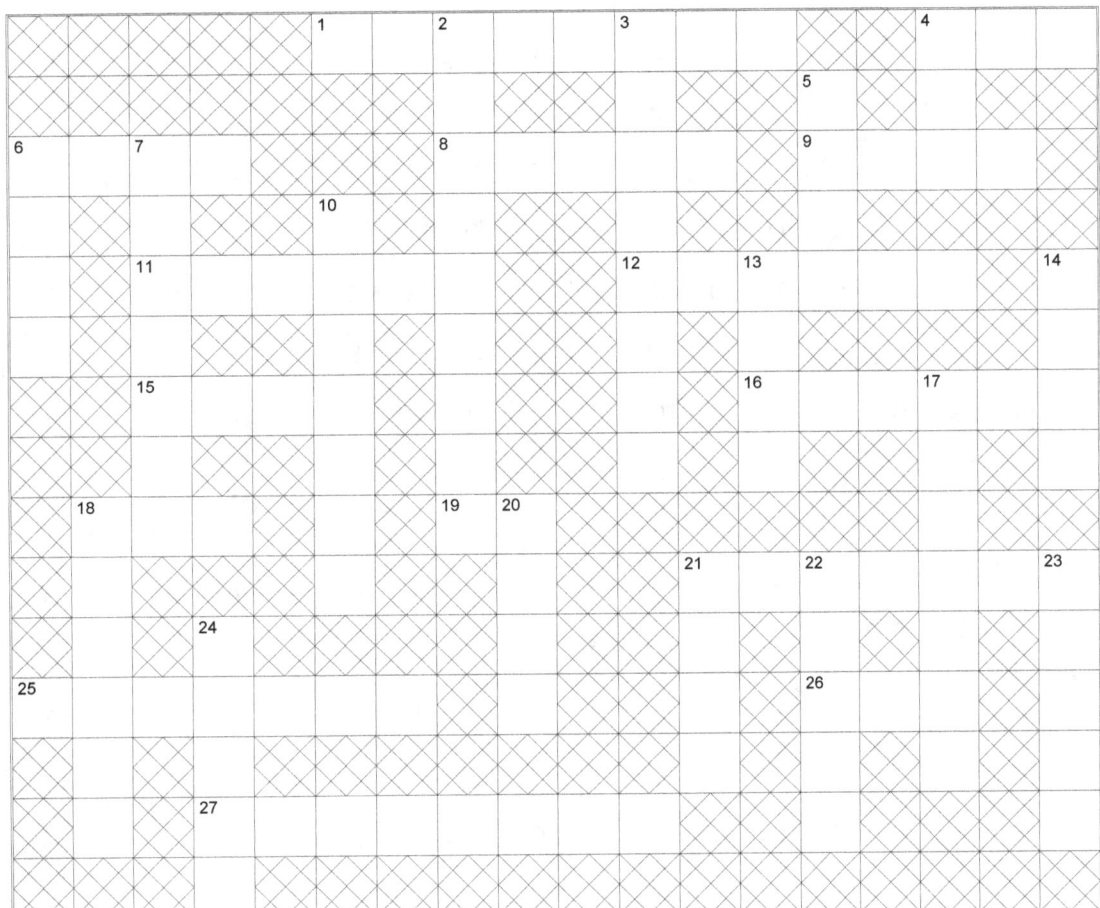

Across
1. Tells of the letter found in Roderigo's pockets
4. 'Yet she must ___, else she'll betray more men.'
6. '___ on, My medicine, ___!'
8. Act division
9. He was passed over for promotion.
11. 'So I will turn her ___ into pitch....'
12. Becomes Lord Governor at the end of the play
15. 'The Moor ... will as tenderly be led by the ___ As asses are.'
16. Iago's wife; Desdemona's servant
18. 'And out of her own goodness make the ___ that shall enmesh them all.'
19. 'I __ not what I __.'
21. Othello to Desdemona
25. 'So please your Grace, my Ancient, a man he is of ___ and trust....'
26. Play division
27. He is love-sick for Desdemona.

Down
2. Othello's wife
3. Emilia said Desdemona was ___.
4. 'Oh, damned Iago! Oh, inhuman __!'
5. Iago told lots of these.
6. Emilia to Iago
7. Iago's motive
10. The jealous Moor
13. 'Men should be what they ___.'
14. Plot; scheme
17. Emilia's ___ to Iago proves stronger than her ___ to Desdemona.
18. '___, I myself. Farewell.'
20. Othello's heritage
21. 'For naught did I in ___, but all in honor.'
22. Othello ___ himself and dies.
23. Iago lied & told Othello Cassio had a ___ in which he cried out to Desdemona.
24. '...you shall more command with ___ Than with your weapons.'

Othello Crossword 3 Answer Key

					1 L	2 D	O	V	3 I	C	O		4 D	I	E
						E			N			5 L		O	
6 W	O	7 R	K			8 S	C	E	N	E		9 I	A	G	O
I		E		10 O		D			O			E			
F		11 V	I	R	T	U	E		12 C	A	13 S	S	I	O	14 P
E		E		H		M			E		E				L
		15 N	O	S	E				N		16 E	M	17 I	L	I A N
		G			L				T		M		O	
	18 N	E	T		L		19 A	20 M					Y		
	O				O			O		21 H	22 U	S	B	A	23 D
	B		24 Y					O		A		T		L	R
25 H	O	N	E	S	T	Y		R		T		26 A	C	T	E
	D		A							E		B		Y	A
	Y	27 R	O	D	E	R	I	G	O			S			M
		S													

Across
1. Tells of the letter found in Roderigo's pockets
4. 'Yet she must ___, else she'll betray more men.'
6. '___ on, My medicine, ___!'
8. Act division
9. He was passed over for promotion.
11. 'So I will turn her ___ into pitch....'
12. Becomes Lord Governor at the end of the play
15. 'The Moor ... will as tenderly be led by the ___ As asses are.'
16. Iago's wife; Desdemona's servant
18. 'And out of her own goodness make the ___ that shall enmesh them all.'
19. 'I __ not what I __.'
21. Othello to Desdemona
25. 'So please your Grace, my Ancient, a man he is of ___ and trust....'
26. Play division
27. He is love-sick for Desdemona.

Down
2. Othello's wife
3. Emilia said Desdemona was ___.
4. 'Oh, damned Iago! Oh, inhuman ___!'
5. Iago told lots of these.
6. Emilia to Iago
7. Iago's motive
10. The jealous Moor
13. 'Men should be what they ___.'
14. Plot; scheme
17. Emilia's ___ to Iago proves stronger than her ___ to Desdemona.
18. '___, I myself. Farewell.'
20. Othello's heritage
21. 'For naught did I in ___, but all in honor.'
22. Othello ___ himself and dies.
23. Iago lied & told Othello Cassio had a ___ in which he cried out to Desdemona.
24. '...you shall more command with ___ Than with your weapons.'

Othello Crossword 4

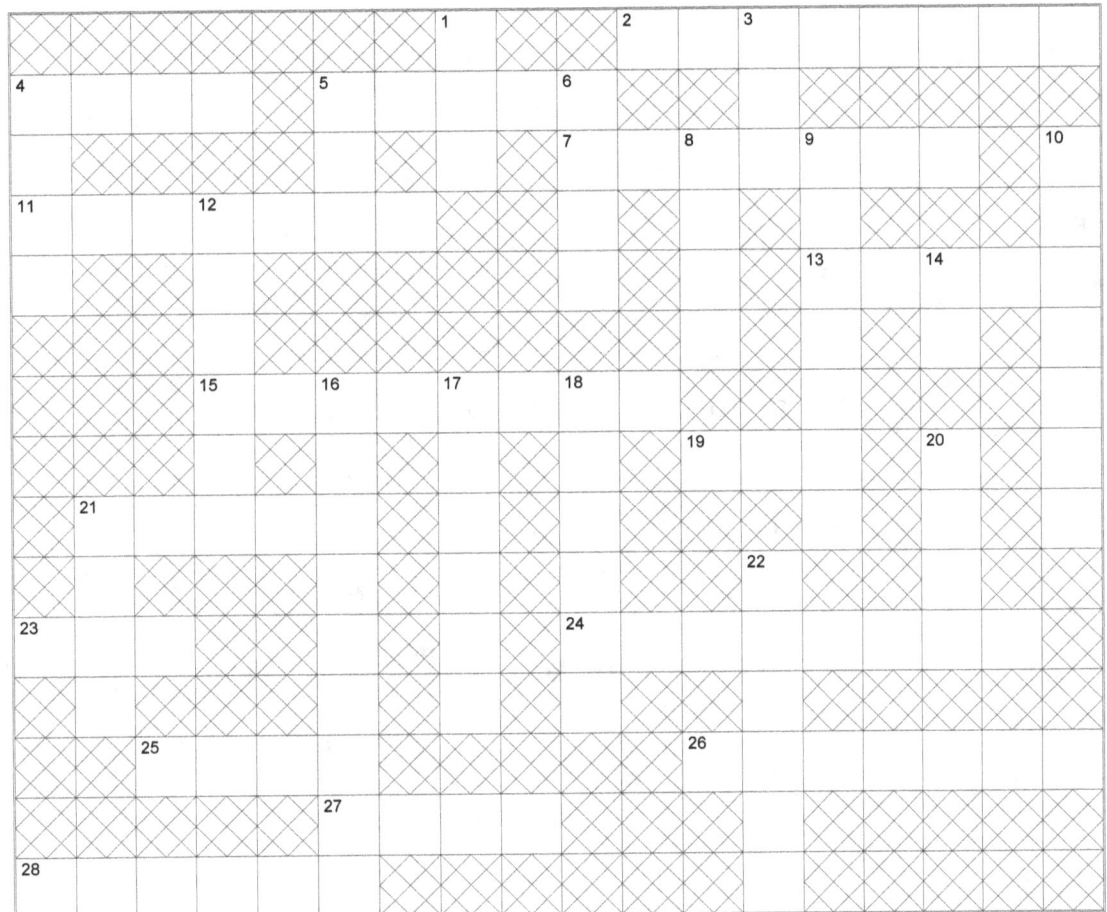

Across
2. He is love-sick for Desdemona.
4. Emilia to Iago
5. Iago lied & told Othello Cassio had a ___ in which he cried out to Desdemona.
7. The jealous Moor
11. Iago's motive
13. '...you shall more command with ___ Than with your weapons.'
15. Tells of the letter found in Roderigo's pockets
19. Play division
21. Othello ___ himself and dies.
23. 'There's magic in the ___ of it.'
24. Emilia said Desdemona was ___.
25. He was passed over for promotion.
26. 'So please your Grace, my Ancient, a man he is of ___ and trust....'
27. 'The Moor ... will as tenderly be led by the ___ As asses are.'
28. Cassio's mistress

Down
1. 'And out of her own goodness make the ___ that shall enmesh them all.'
3. 'Yet she must ___, else she'll betray more men.'
4. '___ on, My medicine, ___!'
5. 'Oh, damned Iago! Oh, inhuman ___!'
6. Othello's heritage
8. 'For naught did I in ___, but all in honor.'
9. Emilia's ___ to Iago proves stronger than her ___ to Desdemona.
10. Othello to Desdemona
12. Iago's wife; Desdemona's servant
14. 'I ___ not what I ___.'
16. Othello's wife
17. 'So I will turn her ___ into pitch....'
18. Becomes Lord Governor at the end of the play
20. Plot; scheme
21. 'Men should be what they ___.'
22. '___, I myself. Farewell.'

Othello Crossword 4 Answer Key

							1 N		2 R	3 D	E	R	I	G	O
4 W	I	F	E		5 D	R	E	6 M		I					
O					O		T	7 O	8 T	H	9 E	L	L	O	10 H
11 R	E	12 V	E	N	G	E		O	H	A	L				U
K		M						R	T		13 Y	E	14 A	R	S
		I						E			A		M		B
		15 L	O	16 D	O	17 V	18 I	C	O		L				A
		I		E		I	A			19 A	C	T	20 P		N
	21 S	T	A	B	S		R		S		Y		L		D
	E			D			T		S	22 N			A		
23 W	E	B		E			U		24 I	N	N	O	C	E	N T
	M			M			E		O		B				
		25 I	A	G	O				26 H	O	N	E	S	T	Y
				27 N	O	S	E				D				
28 B	I	A	N	C	A						Y				

Across
2. He is love-sick for Desdemona.
4. Emilia to Iago
5. Iago lied & told Othello Cassio had a ___ in which he cried out to Desdemona.
7. The jealous Moor
11. Iago's motive
13. '...you shall more command with ___ Than with your weapons.'
15. Tells of the letter found in Roderigo's pockets
19. Play division
21. Othello ___ himself and dies.
23. 'There's magic in the ___ of it.'
24. Emilia said Desdemona was ___.
25. He was passed over for promotion.
26. 'So please your Grace, my Ancient, a man he is of ___ and trust....'
27. 'The Moor ... will as tenderly be led by the ___ As asses are.'
28. Cassio's mistress

Down
1. 'And out of her own goodness make the ___ that shall enmesh them all.'
3. 'Yet she must ___, else she'll betray more men.'
4. '___ on, My medicine, ___!'
5. 'Oh, damned Iago! Oh, inhuman ___!'
6. Othello's heritage
8. 'For naught did I in ___, but all in honor.'
9. Emilia's ___ to Iago proves stronger than her ___ to Desdemona.
10. Othello to Desdemona
12. Iago's wife; Desdemona's servant
14. 'I ___ not what I ___.'
16. Othello's wife
17. 'So I will turn her ___ into pitch....'
18. Becomes Lord Governor at the end of the play
20. Plot; scheme
21. 'Men should be what they ___.'
22. '___, I myself. Farewell.'

Othello

REVENGE	FRIENDSHIP	BIANCA	REPUTATION	CONFESSED
JEALOUSY	AM	DOG	NOBODY	VIRTUE
DREAM	HANDKERCHIEF	FREE SPACE	OTHELLO	LETTERS
JUDGEMENT	SCENE	RODERIGO	HUSBAND	SEEM
WIFE	GRATIANO	DESDEMONA	ACT	EMILIA

Othello

PLAN	SHAKESPEARE	KNAVERY	LIES	MOOR
NOSE	LODOVICO	MURDER	INNOCENT	WEB
HATE	YEARS	FREE SPACE	LOYALTY	DIE
BRABANTIO	WORK	STABS	HONESTY	IAGO
EMILIA	ACT	DESDEMONA	GRATIANO	WIFE

Othello

VIRTUE	NOBODY	DREAM	SHAKESPEARE	JUDGEMENT
OTHELLO	NOSE	REVENGE	HATE	SEEM
LODOVICO	BIANCA	FREE SPACE	PLAN	SCENE
MURDER	HONESTY	LIES	GRATIANO	KNAVERY
WORK	CASSIO	WIFE	DIE	BRABANTIO

Othello

JEALOUSY	RODERIGO	LOYALTY	HUSBAND	ACT
WEB	LETTERS	IAGO	INNOCENT	MOOR
CONFESSED	HANDKERCHIEF	FREE SPACE	AM	NET
REPUTATION	FRIENDSHIP	YEARS	DESDEMONA	EMILIA
BRABANTIO	DIE	WIFE	CASSIO	WORK

Othello

HANDKERCHIEF	REPUTATION	ACT	LETTERS	WEB
IAGO	KNAVERY	BIANCA	HUSBAND	NET
FRIENDSHIP	LOYALTY	FREE SPACE	CASSIO	LIES
DIE	GRATIANO	MURDER	OTHELLO	DREAM
SEEM	AM	REVENGE	JEALOUSY	CONFESSED

Othello

NOSE	BRABANTIO	SCENE	DESDEMONA	HATE
YEARS	JUDGEMENT	INNOCENT	WIFE	WORK
SHAKESPEARE	RODERIGO	FREE SPACE	DOG	VIRTUE
PLAN	HONESTY	LODOVICO	STABS	MOOR
CONFESSED	JEALOUSY	REVENGE	AM	SEEM

Othello

LOYALTY	FRIENDSHIP	JUDGEMENT	YEARS	HANDKERCHIEF
SCENE	LIES	DREAM	MOOR	OTHELLO
LETTERS	WORK	FREE SPACE	EMILIA	WIFE
NOSE	NOBODY	PLAN	BIANCA	HATE
HUSBAND	INNOCENT	DOG	HONESTY	STABS

Othello

DIE	GRATIANO	MURDER	SHAKESPEARE	REPUTATION
RODERIGO	REVENGE	ACT	VIRTUE	KNAVERY
IAGO	DESDEMONA	FREE SPACE	BRABANTIO	NET
JEALOUSY	SEEM	WEB	CONFESSED	LODOVICO
STABS	HONESTY	DOG	INNOCENT	HUSBAND

Othello

MOOR	NET	EMILIA	REVENGE	SHAKESPEARE
BIANCA	FRIENDSHIP	LODOVICO	ACT	KNAVERY
DOG	NOSE	FREE SPACE	JEALOUSY	HATE
OTHELLO	VIRTUE	MURDER	YEARS	HONESTY
LETTERS	CASSIO	JUDGEMENT	AM	LOYALTY

Othello

STABS	PLAN	DESDEMONA	DIE	SCENE
HANDKERCHIEF	SEEM	WORK	NOBODY	REPUTATION
CONFESSED	BRABANTIO	FREE SPACE	WIFE	INNOCENT
IAGO	GRATIANO	LIES	WEB	HUSBAND
LOYALTY	AM	JUDGEMENT	CASSIO	LETTERS

Othello

STABS	RODERIGO	NOSE	LOYALTY	LETTERS
WEB	HANDKERCHIEF	WIFE	DOG	FRIENDSHIP
DESDEMONA	INNOCENT	FREE SPACE	WORK	REVENGE
DIE	SEEM	MOOR	NET	SHAKESPEARE
JUDGEMENT	IAGO	LODOVICO	JEALOUSY	CASSIO

Othello

YEARS	AM	GRATIANO	LIES	OTHELLO
CONFESSED	NOBODY	ACT	KNAVERY	DREAM
VIRTUE	SCENE	FREE SPACE	HONESTY	HUSBAND
PLAN	BRABANTIO	MURDER	REPUTATION	EMILIA
CASSIO	JEALOUSY	LODOVICO	IAGO	JUDGEMENT

Othello

SCENE	RODERIGO	CASSIO	HUSBAND	SEEM
FRIENDSHIP	NET	NOBODY	DOG	BIANCA
IAGO	ACT	FREE SPACE	SHAKESPEARE	JEALOUSY
DESDEMONA	WORK	INNOCENT	BRABANTIO	HATE
LETTERS	KNAVERY	HONESTY	LIES	REPUTATION

Othello

EMILIA	LODOVICO	HANDKERCHIEF	STABS	JUDGEMENT
REVENGE	OTHELLO	GRATIANO	VIRTUE	WEB
AM	YEARS	FREE SPACE	MOOR	CONFESSED
DIE	PLAN	DREAM	MURDER	NOSE
REPUTATION	LIES	HONESTY	KNAVERY	LETTERS

Othello

INNOCENT	SEEM	DOG	HANDKERCHIEF	WEB
MURDER	JEALOUSY	WIFE	LIES	MOOR
WORK	DREAM	FREE SPACE	CASSIO	YEARS
EMILIA	HATE	NOBODY	STABS	OTHELLO
REVENGE	LODOVICO	HONESTY	NOSE	SHAKESPEARE

Othello

VIRTUE	DIE	FRIENDSHIP	LETTERS	HUSBAND
JUDGEMENT	REPUTATION	NET	BRABANTIO	ACT
BIANCA	DESDEMONA	FREE SPACE	LOYALTY	KNAVERY
GRATIANO	PLAN	RODERIGO	IAGO	AM
SHAKESPEARE	NOSE	HONESTY	LODOVICO	REVENGE

Othello

KNAVERY	LOYALTY	LETTERS	WIFE	DREAM
DIE	AM	NOBODY	JUDGEMENT	CASSIO
HUSBAND	HONESTY	FREE SPACE	IAGO	VIRTUE
BRABANTIO	BIANCA	LIES	WORK	MURDER
PLAN	EMILIA	LODOVICO	OTHELLO	YEARS

Othello

NET	REPUTATION	NOSE	HANDKERCHIEF	MOOR
ACT	INNOCENT	DOG	FRIENDSHIP	SCENE
WEB	RODERIGO	FREE SPACE	SEEM	JEALOUSY
SHAKESPEARE	STABS	DESDEMONA	GRATIANO	HATE
YEARS	OTHELLO	LODOVICO	EMILIA	PLAN

Othello

OTHELLO	HONESTY	WEB	IAGO	PLAN
KNAVERY	MOOR	NET	AM	HUSBAND
HANDKERCHIEF	LIES	FREE SPACE	CONFESSED	WIFE
HATE	LETTERS	GRATIANO	YEARS	MURDER
DOG	DREAM	SCENE	BRABANTIO	JUDGEMENT

Othello

BIANCA	DESDEMONA	REVENGE	CASSIO	FRIENDSHIP
VIRTUE	SHAKESPEARE	RODERIGO	STABS	DIE
ACT	INNOCENT	FREE SPACE	LOYALTY	WORK
NOSE	LODOVICO	NOBODY	JEALOUSY	EMILIA
JUDGEMENT	BRABANTIO	SCENE	DREAM	DOG

Othello

DIE	MOOR	NOBODY	CONFESSED	JEALOUSY
KNAVERY	DOG	DESDEMONA	EMILIA	BIANCA
MURDER	SCENE	FREE SPACE	RODERIGO	BRABANTIO
GRATIANO	IAGO	REPUTATION	FRIENDSHIP	WORK
LETTERS	HUSBAND	SEEM	LOYALTY	YEARS

Othello

OTHELLO	ACT	DREAM	NOSE	VIRTUE
LIES	REVENGE	LODOVICO	INNOCENT	HANDKERCHIEF
JUDGEMENT	PLAN	FREE SPACE	SHAKESPEARE	HONESTY
WIFE	STABS	CASSIO	NET	HATE
YEARS	LOYALTY	SEEM	HUSBAND	LETTERS

Othello

DIE	OTHELLO	STABS	BIANCA	PLAN
CASSIO	HUSBAND	JEALOUSY	GRATIANO	DESDEMONA
SCENE	REVENGE	FREE SPACE	MURDER	HONESTY
FRIENDSHIP	VIRTUE	HANDKERCHIEF	WORK	WEB
LIES	CONFESSED	HATE	ACT	DREAM

Othello

INNOCENT	JUDGEMENT	NET	NOBODY	RODERIGO
LOYALTY	YEARS	SHAKESPEARE	EMILIA	NOSE
IAGO	KNAVERY	FREE SPACE	LETTERS	AM
BRABANTIO	DOG	REPUTATION	MOOR	SEEM
DREAM	ACT	HATE	CONFESSED	LIES

Othello

OTHELLO	RODERIGO	HATE	AM	DESDEMONA
BRABANTIO	LIES	FRIENDSHIP	BIANCA	JEALOUSY
CONFESSED	WIFE	FREE SPACE	YEARS	DOG
WORK	REPUTATION	IAGO	MURDER	PLAN
STABS	EMILIA	LETTERS	NOBODY	REVENGE

Othello

DREAM	CASSIO	SHAKESPEARE	GRATIANO	ACT
LODOVICO	SEEM	WEB	HUSBAND	KNAVERY
MOOR	HONESTY	FREE SPACE	VIRTUE	SCENE
JUDGEMENT	INNOCENT	NOSE	NET	LOYALTY
REVENGE	NOBODY	LETTERS	EMILIA	STABS

Othello

RODERIGO	WEB	SCENE	DIE	VIRTUE
LIES	PLAN	WORK	REPUTATION	NOSE
HUSBAND	GRATIANO	FREE SPACE	IAGO	WIFE
HONESTY	LODOVICO	JEALOUSY	YEARS	ACT
LETTERS	HANDKERCHIEF	CONFESSED	BRABANTIO	MOOR

Othello

LOYALTY	BIANCA	MURDER	DESDEMONA	SEEM
AM	REVENGE	EMILIA	JUDGEMENT	NET
KNAVERY	HATE	FREE SPACE	OTHELLO	INNOCENT
SHAKESPEARE	CASSIO	DREAM	DOG	STABS
MOOR	BRABANTIO	CONFESSED	HANDKERCHIEF	LETTERS

Othello

REVENGE	REPUTATION	LODOVICO	WORK	SCENE
MOOR	CASSIO	JUDGEMENT	DOG	SEEM
NOSE	HANDKERCHIEF	FREE SPACE	BIANCA	PLAN
VIRTUE	NET	LETTERS	LIES	YEARS
SHAKESPEARE	BRABANTIO	DREAM	DESDEMONA	RODERIGO

Othello

KNAVERY	WEB	INNOCENT	EMILIA	JEALOUSY
LOYALTY	HONESTY	MURDER	NOBODY	WIFE
IAGO	HUSBAND	FREE SPACE	FRIENDSHIP	STABS
DIE	CONFESSED	OTHELLO	AM	GRATIANO
RODERIGO	DESDEMONA	DREAM	BRABANTIO	SHAKESPEARE

Othello

GRATIANO	MOOR	SHAKESPEARE	HATE	AM
HUSBAND	MURDER	LOYALTY	WIFE	STABS
NET	DREAM	FREE SPACE	DESDEMONA	DIE
YEARS	CASSIO	JUDGEMENT	BIANCA	DOG
REVENGE	VIRTUE	WORK	REPUTATION	HANDKERCHIEF

Othello

NOSE	IAGO	JEALOUSY	KNAVERY	BRABANTIO
INNOCENT	LIES	LETTERS	RODERIGO	OTHELLO
LODOVICO	HONESTY	FREE SPACE	EMILIA	ACT
CONFESSED	FRIENDSHIP	WEB	SEEM	SCENE
HANDKERCHIEF	REPUTATION	WORK	VIRTUE	REVENGE

Othello Vocabulary Word List

No.	Word	Clue/Definition
1.	ADVOCATION	A cause; a path of action
2.	ALACRITY	Eagerness; quickness
3.	ANON	Soon
4.	BASE	Common; low in station
5.	BAWDY	Vulgar; humorously coarse
6.	BEGUILED	Diverted; taken away; also charmed or delighted
7.	BESEECH	Earnestly request
8.	BOMBAST	Puffed-up; pompous
9.	CASTIGATION	Punishment; criticism
10.	CONSPIRE	Secretly plot
11.	CREDULOUS	Gullible
12.	DELUDING	Deceiving
13.	DISMAYED	Having lost courage
14.	EGREGIOUSLY	Conspicuously offensively
15.	EXPOSTULATE	Reason earnestly
16.	FIE	Used to express distaste or disapproval
17.	GRANGE	Farm; granary
18.	GRATIFY	Reward; indulge; satisfy
19.	IMPEDIMENT	Something in the way; a hindrance
20.	IMPORTUNITY	Repeated requests
21.	INCONTINENT	Uncontrolled; unrestrained
22.	INIQUITY	Sin(s)
23.	INSINUATING	Implying; introducing an idea subtlely
24.	LASCIVIOUS	Lecherous
25.	LINGER	To be slow in leaving
26.	MALICE	Spite; ill-will
27.	MANDATE	Command; official instruction
28.	MARS	Damages; marks
29.	OBSEQUIOUS	Fawning; showing servile compliance
30.	PERDITION	Total ruin; damnation
31.	PERIL	Danger
32.	PERNICIOUS	Deadly; destructive
33.	PREFERMENT	Promotion
34.	PROMULGATE	Officially announce
35.	REPROACH	Criticism; disgrace; blame; shame
36.	REQUISITES	Requirements
37.	SATIETY	Condition of being over-filled or over-gratified
38.	SHRIFT	Confessional
39.	SUBORNED	Induced to commit a bad action or perjury
40.	SURFEITED	Fed to excess
41.	TEMPEST	Violent storm
42.	TRIFLE	Something of little importance or value
43.	WIT	Intelligence; humor
44.	WOOED	Courted; dated

Othello Vocabulary Fill In The Blanks 1

_____ 1. Intelligence; humor

_____ 2. Earnestly request

_____ 3. Spite; ill-will

_____ 4. Lecherous

_____ 5. Repeated requests

_____ 6. Common; low in station

_____ 7. Something of little importance or value

_____ 8. Implying; introducing an idea subtlely

_____ 9. Reason earnestly

_____ 10. Reward; indulge; satisfy

_____ 11. Eagerness; quickness

_____ 12. Fed to excess

_____ 13. Puffed-up; pompous

_____ 14. Something in the way; a hindrance

_____ 15. Fawning; showing servile compliance

_____ 16. Damages; marks

_____ 17. Vulgar; humorously coarse

_____ 18. Punishment; criticism

_____ 19. Courted; dated

_____ 20. Soon

Othello Vocabulary Fill In The Blanks 1 Answer Key

WIT	1. Intelligence; humor
BESEECH	2. Earnestly request
MALICE	3. Spite; ill-will
LASCIVIOUS	4. Lecherous
IMPORTUNITY	5. Repeated requests
BASE	6. Common; low in station
TRIFLE	7. Something of little importance or value
INSINUATING	8. Implying; introducing an idea subtlely
EXPOSTULATE	9. Reason earnestly
GRATIFY	10. Reward; indulge; satisfy
ALACRITY	11. Eagerness; quickness
SURFEITED	12. Fed to excess
BOMBAST	13. Puffed-up; pompous
IMPEDIMENT	14. Something in the way; a hindrance
OBSEQUIOUS	15. Fawning; showing servile compliance
MARS	16. Damages; marks
BAWDY	17. Vulgar; humorously coarse
CASTIGATION	18. Punishment; criticism
WOOED	19. Courted; dated
ANON	20. Soon

Othello Vocabulary Fill In The Blanks 2

_____ 1. Uncontrolled; unrestrained

_____ 2. Puffed-up; pompous

_____ 3. Danger

_____ 4. Gullible

_____ 5. A cause; a path of action

_____ 6. Lecherous

_____ 7. Courted; dated

_____ 8. Criticism; disgrace; blame; shame

_____ 9. Deceiving

_____ 10. Something in the way; a hindrance

_____ 11. Requirements

_____ 12. Vulgar; humorously coarse

_____ 13. Diverted; taken away; also charmed or delighted

_____ 14. Confessional

_____ 15. Fawning; showing servile compliance

_____ 16. Fed to excess

_____ 17. Induced to commit a bad action or perjury

_____ 18. To be slow in leaving

_____ 19. Deadly; destructive

_____ 20. Condition of being over-filled or over-gratified

Othello Vocabulary Fill In The Blanks 2 Answer Key

INCONTINENT	1. Uncontrolled; unrestrained
BOMBAST	2. Puffed-up; pompous
PERIL	3. Danger
CREDULOUS	4. Gullible
ADVOCATION	5. A cause; a path of action
LASCIVIOUS	6. Lecherous
WOOED	7. Courted; dated
REPROACH	8. Criticism; disgrace; blame; shame
DELUDING	9. Deceiving
IMPEDIMENT	10. Something in the way; a hindrance
REQUISITES	11. Requirements
BAWDY	12. Vulgar; humorously coarse
BEGUILED	13. Diverted; taken away; also charmed or delighted
SHRIFT	14. Confessional
OBSEQUIOUS	15. Fawning; showing servile compliance
SURFEITED	16. Fed to excess
SUBORNED	17. Induced to commit a bad action or perjury
LINGER	18. To be slow in leaving
PERNICIOUS	19. Deadly; destructive
SATIETY	20. Condition of being over-filled or over-gratified

Othello Vocabulary Fill In The Blanks 3

1. Having lost courage
2. Diverted; taken away; also charmed or delighted
3. Soon
4. Courted; dated
5. Deceiving
6. Secretly plot
7. Condition of being over-filled or over-gratified
8. Intelligence; humor
9. Conspicuously offensively
10. Command; official instruction
11. Violent storm
12. Requirements
13. Something in the way; a hindrance
14. Vulgar; humorously coarse
15. Sin(s)
16. Total ruin; damnation
17. Eagerness; quickness
18. Implying; introducing an idea subtlely
19. Spite; ill-will
20. Reason earnestly

Othello Vocabulary Fill In The Blanks 3 Answer Key

DISMAYED	1. Having lost courage
BEGUILED	2. Diverted; taken away; also charmed or delighted
ANON	3. Soon
WOOED	4. Courted; dated
DELUDING	5. Deceiving
CONSPIRE	6. Secretly plot
SATIETY	7. Condition of being over-filled or over-gratified
WIT	8. Intelligence; humor
EGREGIOUSLY	9. Conspicuously offensively
MANDATE	10. Command; official instruction
TEMPEST	11. Violent storm
REQUISITES	12. Requirements
IMPEDIMENT	13. Something in the way; a hindrance
BAWDY	14. Vulgar; humorously coarse
INIQUITY	15. Sin(s)
PERDITION	16. Total ruin; damnation
ALACRITY	17. Eagerness; quickness
INSINUATING	18. Implying; introducing an idea subtlely
MALICE	19. Spite; ill-will
EXPOSTULATE	20. Reason earnestly

Othello Vocabulary Fill In The Blanks 4

_____ 1. Uncontrolled; unrestrained

_____ 2. Danger

_____ 3. Conspicuously offensively

_____ 4. Secretly plot

_____ 5. Spite; ill-will

_____ 6. Criticism; disgrace; blame; shame

_____ 7. Total ruin; damnation

_____ 8. Something of little importance or value

_____ 9. Reward; indulge; satisfy

_____ 10. Having lost courage

_____ 11. Used to express distaste or disapproval

_____ 12. Confessional

_____ 13. Condition of being over-filled or over-gratified

_____ 14. Intelligence; humor

_____ 15. Induced to commit a bad action or perjury

_____ 16. Something in the way; a hindrance

_____ 17. To be slow in leaving

_____ 18. Implying; introducing an idea subtlely

_____ 19. Lecherous

_____ 20. Diverted; taken away; also charmed or delighted

Othello Vocabulary Fill In The Blanks 4 Answer Key

INCONTINENT	1. Uncontrolled; unrestrained
PERIL	2. Danger
EGREGIOUSLY	3. Conspicuously offensively
CONSPIRE	4. Secretly plot
MALICE	5. Spite; ill-will
REPROACH	6. Criticism; disgrace; blame; shame
PERDITION	7. Total ruin; damnation
TRIFLE	8. Something of little importance or value
GRATIFY	9. Reward; indulge; satisfy
DISMAYED	10. Having lost courage
FIE	11. Used to express distaste or disapproval
SHRIFT	12. Confessional
SATIETY	13. Condition of being over-filled or over-gratified
WIT	14. Intelligence; humor
SUBORNED	15. Induced to commit a bad action or perjury
IMPEDIMENT	16. Something in the way; a hindrance
LINGER	17. To be slow in leaving
INSINUATING	18. Implying; introducing an idea subtlely
LASCIVIOUS	19. Lecherous
BEGUILED	20. Diverted; taken away; also charmed or delighted

Othello Vocabulary Matching 1

___ 1. SATIETY A. Common; low in station
___ 2. WOOED B. A cause; a path of action
___ 3. OBSEQUIOUS C. Soon
___ 4. BASE D. Induced to commit a bad action or perjury
___ 5. EXPOSTULATE E. Intelligence; humor
___ 6. BAWDY F. Eagerness; quickness
___ 7. LINGER G. Secretly plot
___ 8. MANDATE H. Command; official instruction
___ 9. PERIL I. Lecherous
___10. PERDITION J. Deceiving
___11. ADVOCATION K. Having lost courage
___12. ALACRITY L. Requirements
___13. SURFEITED M. Courted; dated
___14. CONSPIRE N. Violent storm
___15. INSINUATING O. Vulgar; humorously coarse
___16. REQUISITES P. Promotion
___17. DISMAYED Q. Total ruin; damnation
___18. WIT R. To be slow in leaving
___19. TEMPEST S. Danger
___20. DELUDING T. Fawning; showing servile compliance
___21. LASCIVIOUS U. Criticism; disgrace; blame; shame
___22. PREFERMENT V. Implying; introducing an idea subtlely
___23. ANON W. Fed to excess
___24. SUBORNED X. Condition of being over-filled or over-gratified
___25. REPROACH Y. Reason earnestly

Othello Vocabulary Matching 1 Answer Key

X - 1. SATIETY
M - 2. WOOED
T - 3. OBSEQUIOUS
A - 4. BASE
Y - 5. EXPOSTULATE
O - 6. BAWDY
R - 7. LINGER
H - 8. MANDATE
S - 9. PERIL
Q - 10. PERDITION
B - 11. ADVOCATION
F - 12. ALACRITY
W - 13. SURFEITED
G - 14. CONSPIRE
V - 15. INSINUATING
L - 16. REQUISITES
K - 17. DISMAYED
E - 18. WIT
N - 19. TEMPEST
J - 20. DELUDING
I - 21. LASCIVIOUS
P - 22. PREFERMENT
C - 23. ANON
D - 24. SUBORNED
U - 25. REPROACH

A. Common; low in station
B. A cause; a path of action
C. Soon
D. Induced to commit a bad action or perjury
E. Intelligence; humor
F. Eagerness; quickness
G. Secretly plot
H. Command; official instruction
I. Lecherous
J. Deceiving
K. Having lost courage
L. Requirements
M. Courted; dated
N. Violent storm
O. Vulgar; humorously coarse
P. Promotion
Q. Total ruin; damnation
R. To be slow in leaving
S. Danger
T. Fawning; showing servile compliance
U. Criticism; disgrace; blame; shame
V. Implying; introducing an idea subtlely
W. Fed to excess
X. Condition of being over-filled or over-gratified
Y. Reason earnestly

Othello Vocabulary Matching 2

___ 1. DISMAYED   A. Common; low in station
___ 2. DELUDING   B. Conspicuously offensively
___ 3. INCONTINENT   C. Something of little importance or value
___ 4. TEMPEST   D. Deceiving
___ 5. IMPEDIMENT   E. Lecherous
___ 6. BOMBAST   F. A cause; a path of action
___ 7. MANDATE   G. Having lost courage
___ 8. PERNICIOUS   H. Uncontrolled; unrestrained
___ 9. MALICE   I. Repeated requests
___10. ANON   J. Implying; introducing an idea subtlely
___11. IMPORTUNITY   K. Reason earnestly
___12. ALACRITY   L. Puffed-up; pompous
___13. PERIL   M. Punishment; criticism
___14. EXPOSTULATE   N. Spite; ill-will
___15. LASCIVIOUS   O. Requirements
___16. EGREGIOUSLY   P. Promotion
___17. ADVOCATION   Q. Command; official instruction
___18. REQUISITES   R. Danger
___19. TRIFLE   S. Violent storm
___20. INSINUATING   T. Eagerness; quickness
___21. PREFERMENT   U. Total ruin; damnation
___22. BASE   V. Soon
___23. SURFEITED   W. Deadly; destructive
___24. CASTIGATION   X. Fed to excess
___25. PERDITION   Y. Something in the way; a hindrance

Othello Vocabulary Matching 2 Answer Key

G - 1. DISMAYED	A.	Common; low in station
D - 2. DELUDING	B.	Conspicuously offensively
H - 3. INCONTINENT	C.	Something of little importance or value
S - 4. TEMPEST	D.	Deceiving
Y - 5. IMPEDIMENT	E.	Lecherous
L - 6. BOMBAST	F.	A cause; a path of action
Q - 7. MANDATE	G.	Having lost courage
W - 8. PERNICIOUS	H.	Uncontrolled; unrestrained
N - 9. MALICE	I.	Repeated requests
V - 10. ANON	J.	Implying; introducing an idea subtlely
I - 11. IMPORTUNITY	K.	Reason earnestly
T - 12. ALACRITY	L.	Puffed-up; pompous
R - 13. PERIL	M.	Punishment; criticism
K - 14. EXPOSTULATE	N.	Spite; ill-will
E - 15. LASCIVIOUS	O.	Requirements
B - 16. EGREGIOUSLY	P.	Promotion
F - 17. ADVOCATION	Q.	Command; official instruction
O - 18. REQUISITES	R.	Danger
C - 19. TRIFLE	S.	Violent storm
J - 20. INSINUATING	T.	Eagerness; quickness
P - 21. PREFERMENT	U.	Total ruin; damnation
A - 22. BASE	V.	Soon
X - 23. SURFEITED	W.	Deadly; destructive
M - 24. CASTIGATION	X.	Fed to excess
U - 25. PERDITION	Y.	Something in the way; a hindrance

Othello Vocabulary Matching 3

___ 1. OBSEQUIOUS A. Courted; dated
___ 2. IMPORTUNITY B. Reason earnestly
___ 3. LINGER C. Induced to commit a bad action or perjury
___ 4. REPROACH D. Fed to excess
___ 5. EGREGIOUSLY E. A cause; a path of action
___ 6. LASCIVIOUS F. Secretly plot
___ 7. SURFEITED G. Confessional
___ 8. EXPOSTULATE H. To be slow in leaving
___ 9. WIT I. Requirements
___10. MARS J. Violent storm
___11. GRANGE K. Gullible
___12. CREDULOUS L. Farm; granary
___13. SUBORNED M. Eagerness; quickness
___14. FIE N. Conspicuously offensively
___15. REQUISITES O. Intelligence; humor
___16. WOOED P. Something in the way; a hindrance
___17. CONSPIRE Q. Damages; marks
___18. SHRIFT R. Soon
___19. INIQUITY S. Criticism; disgrace; blame; shame
___20. TEMPEST T. Repeated requests
___21. ADVOCATION U. Sin(s)
___22. IMPEDIMENT V. Puffed-up; pompous
___23. ALACRITY W. Fawning; showing servile compliance
___24. BOMBAST X. Used to express distaste or disapproval
___25. ANON Y. Lecherous

Othello Vocabulary Matching 3 Answer Key

W - 1.	OBSEQUIOUS	A. Courted; dated
T - 2.	IMPORTUNITY	B. Reason earnestly
H - 3.	LINGER	C. Induced to commit a bad action or perjury
S - 4.	REPROACH	D. Fed to excess
N - 5.	EGREGIOUSLY	E. A cause; a path of action
Y - 6.	LASCIVIOUS	F. Secretly plot
D - 7.	SURFEITED	G. Confessional
B - 8.	EXPOSTULATE	H. To be slow in leaving
O - 9.	WIT	I. Requirements
Q -10.	MARS	J. Violent storm
L -11.	GRANGE	K. Gullible
K -12.	CREDULOUS	L. Farm; granary
C -13.	SUBORNED	M. Eagerness; quickness
X -14.	FIE	N. Conspicuously offensively
I -15.	REQUISITES	O. Intelligence; humor
A -16.	WOOED	P. Something in the way; a hindrance
F -17.	CONSPIRE	Q. Damages; marks
G -18.	SHRIFT	R. Soon
U -19.	INIQUITY	S. Criticism; disgrace; blame; shame
J -20.	TEMPEST	T. Repeated requests
E -21.	ADVOCATION	U. Sin(s)
P -22.	IMPEDIMENT	V. Puffed-up; pompous
M -23.	ALACRITY	W. Fawning; showing servile compliance
V -24.	BOMBAST	X. Used to express distaste or disapproval
R -25.	ANON	Y. Lecherous

Othello Vocabulary Matching 4

___ 1. BASE
___ 2. INSINUATING
___ 3. MALICE
___ 4. REPROACH
___ 5. ADVOCATION
___ 6. REQUISITES
___ 7. TEMPEST
___ 8. SURFEITED
___ 9. PREFERMENT
___10. OBSEQUIOUS
___11. SHRIFT
___12. WIT
___13. GRATIFY
___14. CREDULOUS
___15. WOOED
___16. EGREGIOUSLY
___17. BESEECH
___18. IMPORTUNITY
___19. TRIFLE
___20. PERDITION
___21. IMPEDIMENT
___22. PERNICIOUS
___23. ANON
___24. EXPOSTULATE
___25. PERIL

A. Requirements
B. Earnestly request
C. Something of little importance or value
D. Total ruin; damnation
E. Confessional
F. Violent storm
G. Promotion
H. Common; low in station
I. Reason earnestly
J. Something in the way; a hindrance
K. Criticism; disgrace; blame; shame
L. Gullible
M. Conspicuously offensively
N. Fed to excess
O. Fawning; showing servile compliance
P. Courted; dated
Q. Danger
R. Implying; introducing an idea subtlely
S. Deadly; destructive
T. Spite; ill-will
U. Intelligence; humor
V. A cause; a path of action
W. Reward; indulge; satisfy
X. Soon
Y. Repeated requests

Othello Vocabulary Matching 4 Answer Key

H - 1.	BASE	A.	Requirements
R - 2.	INSINUATING	B.	Earnestly request
T - 3.	MALICE	C.	Something of little importance or value
K - 4.	REPROACH	D.	Total ruin; damnation
V - 5.	ADVOCATION	E.	Confessional
A - 6.	REQUISITES	F.	Violent storm
F - 7.	TEMPEST	G.	Promotion
N - 8.	SURFEITED	H.	Common; low in station
G - 9.	PREFERMENT	I.	Reason earnestly
O - 10.	OBSEQUIOUS	J.	Something in the way; a hindrance
E - 11.	SHRIFT	K.	Criticism; disgrace; blame; shame
U - 12.	WIT	L.	Gullible
W - 13.	GRATIFY	M.	Conspicuously offensively
L - 14.	CREDULOUS	N.	Fed to excess
P - 15.	WOOED	O.	Fawning; showing servile compliance
M - 16.	EGREGIOUSLY	P.	Courted; dated
B - 17.	BESEECH	Q.	Danger
Y - 18.	IMPORTUNITY	R.	Implying; introducing an idea subtlely
C - 19.	TRIFLE	S.	Deadly; destructive
D - 20.	PERDITION	T.	Spite; ill-will
J - 21.	IMPEDIMENT	U.	Intelligence; humor
S - 22.	PERNICIOUS	V.	A cause; a path of action
X - 23.	ANON	W.	Reward; indulge; satisfy
I - 24.	EXPOSTULATE	X.	Soon
Q - 25.	PERIL	Y.	Repeated requests

Othello Vocabulary Magic Squares 1

Match the definition with the vocabulary word. Put your answers in the magic squares below. When your answers are correct, all columns and rows will add to the same number.

A. IMPEDIMENT E. CREDULOUS I. ANON M. BOMBAST
B. TEMPEST F. SATIETY J. REPROACH N. ALACRITY
C. FIE G. LINGER K. WOOED O. EGREGIOUSLY
D. CONSPIRE H. PERIL L. DISMAYED P. INCONTINENT

1. Something in the way; a hindrance
2. Eagerness; quickness
3. Criticism; disgrace; blame; shame
4. Gullible
5. To be slow in leaving
6. Having lost courage
7. Uncontrolled; unrestrained
8. Used to express distaste or disapproval
9. Conspicuously offensively
10. Secretly plot
11. Danger
12. Courted; dated
13. Soon
14. Condition of being over-filled or over-gratified
15. Violent storm
16. Puffed-up; pompous

A=	B=	C=	D=
E=	F=	G=	H=
I=	J=	K=	L=
M=	N=	O=	P=

Othello Vocabulary Magic Squares 1 Answer Key

Match the definition with the vocabulary word. Put your answers in the magic squares below. When your answers are correct, all columns and rows will add to the same number.

A. IMPEDIMENT
B. TEMPEST
C. FIE
D. CONSPIRE
E. CREDULOUS
F. SATIETY
G. LINGER
H. PERIL
I. ANON
J. REPROACH
K. WOOED
L. DISMAYED
M. BOMBAST
N. ALACRITY
O. EGREGIOUSLY
P. INCONTINENT

1. Something in the way; a hindrance
2. Eagerness; quickness
3. Criticism; disgrace; blame; shame
4. Gullible
5. To be slow in leaving
6. Having lost courage
7. Uncontrolled; unrestrained
8. Used to express distaste or disapproval
9. Conspicuously offensively
10. Secretly plot
11. Danger
12. Courted; dated
13. Soon
14. Condition of being over-filled or over-gratified
15. Violent storm
16. Puffed-up; pompous

A=1	B=15	C=8	D=10
E=4	F=14	G=5	H=11
I=13	J=3	K=12	L=6
M=16	N=2	O=9	P=7

Othello Vocabulary Magic Squares 2

Match the definition with the vocabulary word. Put your answers in the magic squares below. When your answers are correct, all columns and rows will add to the same number.

A. FIE
B. CASTIGATION
C. INIQUITY
D. BESEECH
E. SUBORNED
F. GRATIFY
G. IMPORTUNITY
H. EXPOSTULATE
I. SURFEITED
J. SATIETY
K. LASCIVIOUS
L. GRANGE
M. ANON
N. WOOED
O. LINGER
P. TEMPEST

1. Punishment; criticism
2. Repeated requests
3. Lecherous
4. Courted; dated
5. Soon
6. Farm; granary
7. Reason earnestly
8. Used to express distaste or disapproval
9. Violent storm
10. Fed to excess
11. Induced to commit a bad action or perjury
12. Earnestly request
13. Sin(s)
14. Reward; indulge; satisfy
15. Condition of being over-filled or over-gratified
16. To be slow in leaving

A=	B=	C=	D=
E=	F=	G=	H=
I=	J=	K=	L=
M=	N=	O=	P=

Othello Vocabulary Magic Squares 2 Answer Key

Match the definition with the vocabulary word. Put your answers in the magic squares below. When your answers are correct, all columns and rows will add to the same number.

A. FIE
B. CASTIGATION
C. INIQUITY
D. BESEECH
E. SUBORNED
F. GRATIFY
G. IMPORTUNITY
H. EXPOSTULATE
I. SURFEITED
J. SATIETY
K. LASCIVIOUS
L. GRANGE
M. ANON
N. WOOED
O. LINGER
P. TEMPEST

1. Punishment; criticism
2. Repeated requests
3. Lecherous
4. Courted; dated
5. Soon
6. Farm; granary
7. Reason earnestly
8. Used to express distaste or disapproval
9. Violent storm
10. Fed to excess
11. Induced to commit a bad action or perjury
12. Earnestly request
13. Sin(s)
14. Reward; indulge; satisfy
15. Condition of being over-filled or over-gratified
16. To be slow in leaving

A=8	B=1	C=13	D=12
E=11	F=14	G=2	H=7
I=10	J=15	K=3	L=6
M=5	N=4	O=16	P=9

Othello Vocabulary Magic Squares 3

Match the definition with the vocabulary word. Put your answers in the magic squares below. When your answers are correct, all columns and rows will add to the same number.

A. EXPOSTULATE   E. LASCIVIOUS   I. ANON   M. IMPEDIMENT
B. IMPORTUNITY   F. SATIETY   J. FIE   N. PROMULGATE
C. SURFEITED   G. OBSEQUIOUS   K. CONSPIRE   O. DELUDING
D. SHRIFT   H. ALACRITY   L. INIQUITY   P. LINGER

1. Officially announce
2. Fawning; showing servile compliance
3. Sin(s)
4. Reason earnestly
5. Secretly plot
6. Repeated requests
7. Something in the way; a hindrance
8. Eagerness; quickness
9. Lecherous
10. To be slow in leaving
11. Fed to excess
12. Used to express distaste or disapproval
13. Confessional
14. Soon
15. Condition of being over-filled or over-gratified
16. Deceiving

A=	B=	C=	D=
E=	F=	G=	H=
I=	J=	K=	L=
M=	N=	O=	P=

Othello Vocabulary Magic Squares 3 Answer Key

Match the definition with the vocabulary word. Put your answers in the magic squares below. When your answers are correct, all columns and rows will add to the same number.

A. EXPOSTULATE   E. LASCIVIOUS   I. ANON   M. IMPEDIMENT
B. IMPORTUNITY   F. SATIETY   J. FIE   N. PROMULGATE
C. SURFEITED   G. OBSEQUIOUS   K. CONSPIRE   O. DELUDING
D. SHRIFT   H. ALACRITY   L. INIQUITY   P. LINGER

1. Officially announce
2. Fawning; showing servile compliance
3. Sin(s)
4. Reason earnestly
5. Secretly plot
6. Repeated requests
7. Something in the way; a hindrance
8. Eagerness; quickness
9. Lecherous
10. To be slow in leaving
11. Fed to excess
12. Used to express distaste or disapproval
13. Confessional
14. Soon
15. Condition of being over-filled or over-gratified
16. Deceiving

A=4	B=6	C=11	D=13
E=9	F=15	G=2	H=8
I=14	J=12	K=5	L=3
M=7	N=1	O=16	P=10

Othello Vocabulary Magic Squares 4

Match the definition with the vocabulary word. Put your answers in the magic squares below. When your answers are correct, all columns and rows will add to the same number.

A. PERIL
B. SUBORNED
C. SURFEITED
D. OBSEQUIOUS
E. PROMULGATE
F. GRANGE
G. BAWDY
H. EGREGIOUSLY
I. DISMAYED
J. WIT
K. MARS
L. WOOED
M. CASTIGATION
N. INIQUITY
O. MALICE
P. DELUDING

1. Conspicuously offensively
2. Punishment; criticism
3. Induced to commit a bad action or perjury
4. Damages; marks
5. Intelligence; humor
6. Fed to excess
7. Deceiving
8. Officially announce
9. Spite; ill-will
10. Farm; granary
11. Having lost courage
12. Fawning; showing servile compliance
13. Danger
14. Courted; dated
15. Vulgar; humorously coarse
16. Sin(s)

A=	B=	C=	D=
E=	F=	G=	H=
I=	J=	K=	L=
M=	N=	O=	P=

Othello Vocabulary Magic Squares 4 Answer Key

Match the definition with the vocabulary word. Put your answers in the magic squares below. When your answers are correct, all columns and rows will add to the same number.

A. PERIL	E. PROMULGATE	I. DISMAYED	M. CASTIGATION
B. SUBORNED	F. GRANGE	J. WIT	N. INIQUITY
C. SURFEITED	G. BAWDY	K. MARS	O. MALICE
D. OBSEQUIOUS	H. EGREGIOUSLY	L. WOOED	P. DELUDING

1. Conspicuously offensively
2. Punishment; criticism
3. Induced to commit a bad action or perjury
4. Damages; marks
5. Intelligence; humor
6. Fed to excess
7. Deceiving
8. Officially announce
9. Spite; ill-will
10. Farm; granary
11. Having lost courage
12. Fawning; showing servile compliance
13. Danger
14. Courted; dated
15. Vulgar; humorously coarse
16. Sin(s)

A=13	B=3	C=6	D=12
E=8	F=10	G=15	H=1
I=11	J=5	K=4	L=14
M=2	N=16	O=9	P=7

Othello Vocabulary Word Search 1

Words are placed backwards, forward, diagonally, up and down. Clues listed below can help you find the words. Circle the hidden vocabulary words in the maze.

```
E P H X Y S B P V S E T I S I U Q E R
G R N C Z U O E D S U O I U Q E S B O
R O O O T O M R W L A R R W N M J D I
E M I N E I B D A P G L F V V H S F M
G U T S M V A I D R R M A E H K A Q P
I L A P P I S T V N A X D C I D T B O
O G G I E C T I O W T L J P R T I A R
U A I R S S M O C M I S T E W I E W T
S T T E T A D N A M F S H R I F T D U
L E S G I L O R T W Y J E I I N Y Y N
Y A A N W N S R I R R G L L E F Y B I
B P C A A K E B O W N C K M M C L D T
R S P R Y I D T N I H N R B F R D E Y
G Y U G F G N C L C V E S E M E E Y P
R S G B R L X I A K F F L C L D L A F
S D E O O W W O Q E T W N I D U U M J
Q P Z K F R R D R U K G U L H L D S Z
K W C T R P N P V R I G W A Q O I I R
B E S E E C H E F P E T N M J U N D K
D W D R C G T Q D B R K Y F D S G N P
```

A cause; a path of action (10)
Command; official instruction (7)
Common; low in station (4)
Condition of being over-filled or over-gratified (7)
Confessional (6)
Conspicuously offensively (11)
Courted; dated (5)
Criticism; disgrace; blame; shame (8)
Damages; marks (4)
Danger (5)
Deceiving (8)
Diverted; taken away; also charmed or delighted (8)
Eagerness; quickness (8)
Earnestly request (7)
Farm; granary (6)
Fawning; showing servile compliance (10)
Fed to excess (9)
Gullible (9)
Having lost courage (8)

Induced to commit a bad action or perjury (8)
Intelligence; humor (3)
Lecherous (10)
Officially announce (10)
Promotion (10)
Puffed-up; pompous (7)
Punishment; criticism (11)
Repeated requests (11)
Requirements (10)
Reward; indulge; satisfy (7)
Secretly plot (8)
Sin(s) (8)
Something of little importance or value (6)
Soon (4)
Spite; ill-will (6)
To be slow in leaving (6)
Total ruin; damnation (9)
Used to express distaste or disapproval (3)
Violent storm (7)
Vulgar; humorously coarse (5)

Othello Vocabulary Word Search 1 Answer Key

Words are placed backwards, forward, diagonally, up and down. Clues listed below can help you find the words. Circle the hidden vocabulary words in the maze.

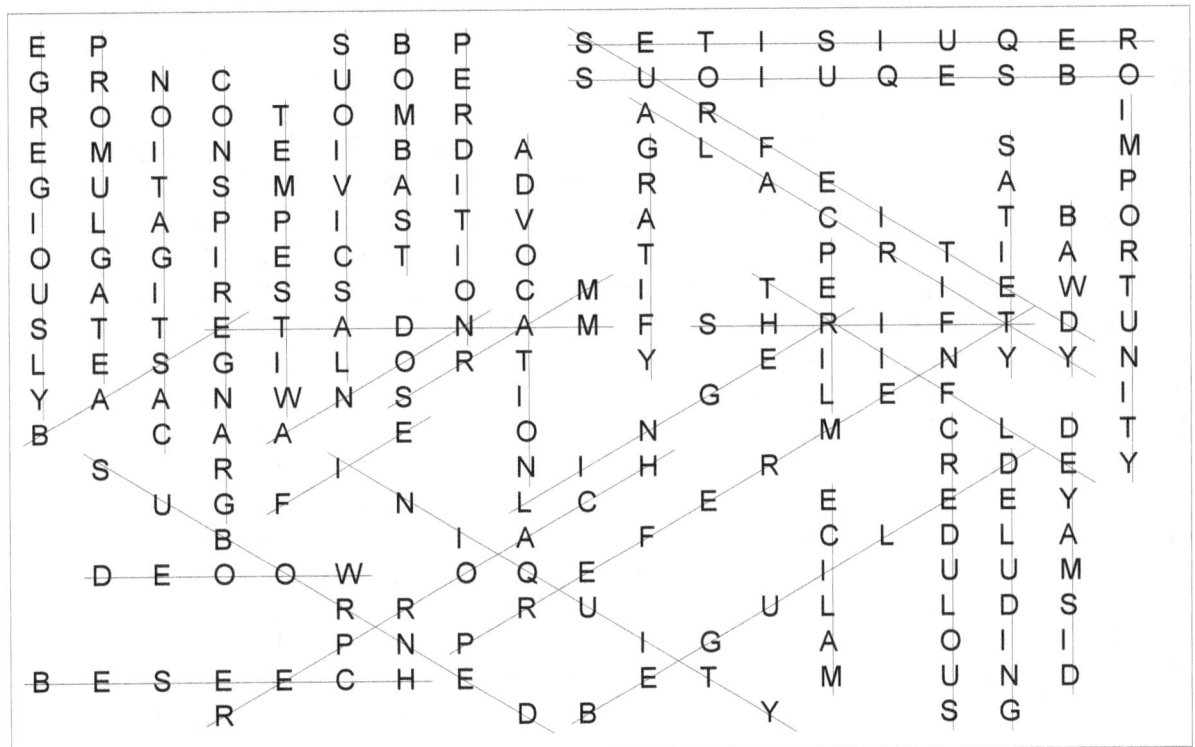

A cause; a path of action (10)
Command; official instruction (7)
Common; low in station (4)
Condition of being over-filled or over-gratified (7)
Confessional (6)
Conspicuously offensively (11)
Courted; dated (5)
Criticism; disgrace; blame; shame (8)
Damages; marks (4)
Danger (5)
Deceiving (8)
Diverted; taken away; also charmed or delighted (8)
Eagerness; quickness (8)
Earnestly request (7)
Farm; granary (6)
Fawning; showing servile compliance (10)
Fed to excess (9)
Gullible (9)
Having lost courage (8)

Induced to commit a bad action or perjury (8)
Intelligence; humor (3)
Lecherous (10)
Officially announce (10)
Promotion (10)
Puffed-up; pompous (7)
Punishment; criticism (11)
Repeated requests (11)
Requirements (10)
Reward; indulge; satisfy (7)
Secretly plot (8)
Sin(s) (8)
Something of little importance or value (6)
Soon (4)
Spite; ill-will (6)
To be slow in leaving (6)
Total ruin; damnation (9)
Used to express distaste or disapproval (3)
Violent storm (7)
Vulgar; humorously coarse (5)

Othello Vocabulary Word Search 2

Words are placed backwards, forward, diagonally, up and down. Clues listed below can help you find the words. Circle the hidden vocabulary words in the maze.

```
R P G R A T I F Y K S K M B G W D I J
E R P R O M U L G A T E B A W D Y M Z
P E H F Z G I D B N N E X S N I Y P G
R F F T Y R E S E O E Y M E D D T O G
O E T N E L J N N I M O Q P F N A R S
A R G P U N I O H N I B F I E J M T B
C M V D Q T I C S I D S A H S S C U E
H E I G N T E C U Q E E T S A K T N H
H N G O I E X T B U P Q H R T T F I Z
G T C D S R A M O I M U P A I G Y T I
K N R E H I Q A R T I I N G E F K Y N
I E B D R P Z L N Y S O T R T S L D S
P L Q M I S R I E B N U M A Y F E E I
M J I R F N P C D Q E S F N D T W V N
R B K N T O W E W T Q G Y G I W O D U
P G N H G C S N Q X J F U E H Q O R A
J N X C R E D U L O U S F I K C E M T
X X A L A C R I T Y P R N H L D D Q I
P E R N I C I O U S U G P K S E B X N
D I S M A Y E D K S L X V K M L D D G
```

Command; official instruction (7)
Common; low in station (4)
Condition of being over-filled or over-gratified (7)
Confessional (6)
Courted; dated (5)
Criticism; disgrace; blame; shame (8)
Damages; marks (4)
Danger (5)
Deadly; destructive (10)
Deceiving (8)
Diverted; taken away; also charmed or delighted (8)
Eagerness; quickness (8)
Earnestly request (7)
Farm; granary (6)
Fawning; showing servile compliance (10)
Fed to excess (9)
Gullible (9)
Having lost courage (8)
Implying; introducing an idea subtlely (11)

Induced to commit a bad action or perjury (8)
Intelligence; humor (3)
Officially announce (10)
Promotion (10)
Puffed-up; pompous (7)
Repeated requests (11)
Reward; indulge; satisfy (7)
Secretly plot (8)
Sin(s) (8)
Something in the way; a hindrance (10)
Something of little importance or value (6)
Soon (4)
Spite; ill-will (6)
To be slow in leaving (6)
Total ruin; damnation (9)
Uncontrolled; unrestrained (11)
Used to express distaste or disapproval (3)
Violent storm (7)
Vulgar; humorously coarse (5)

Othello Vocabulary Word Search 2 Answer Key

Words are placed backwards, forward, diagonally, up and down. Clues listed below can help you find the words. Circle the hidden vocabulary words in the maze.

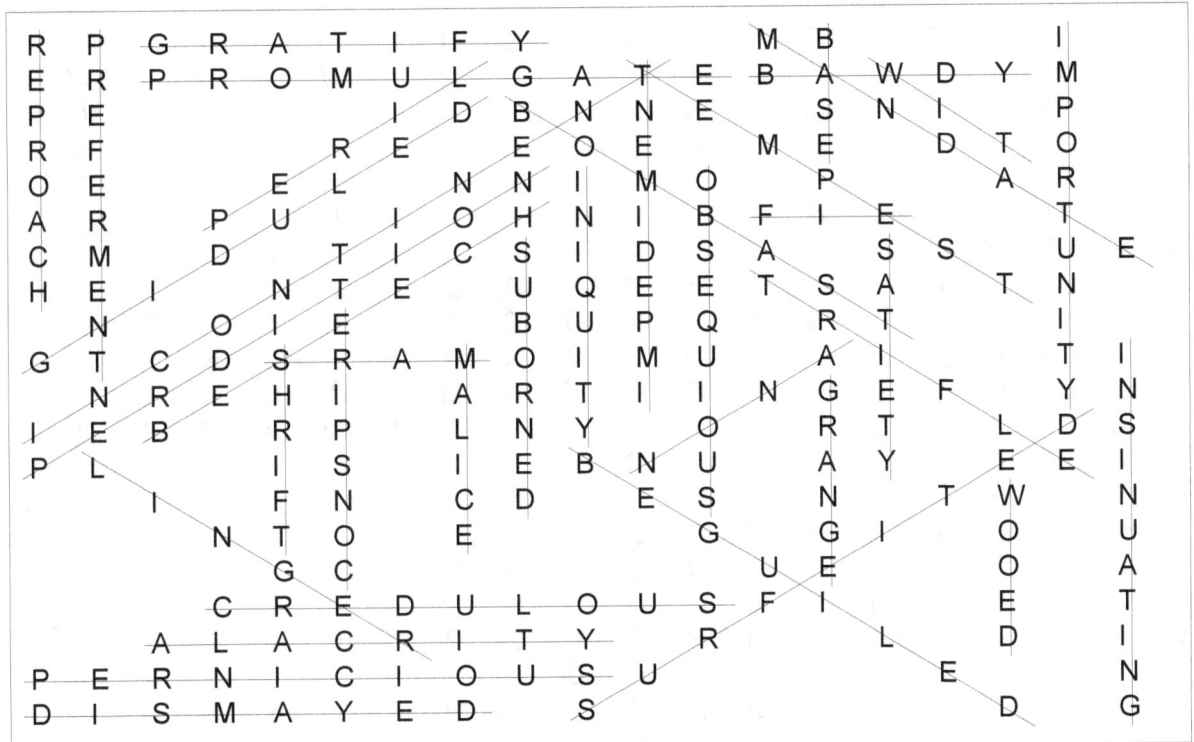

Command; official instruction (7)
Common; low in station (4)
Condition of being over-filled or over-gratified (7)
Confessional (6)
Courted; dated (5)
Criticism; disgrace; blame; shame (8)
Damages; marks (4)
Danger (5)
Deadly; destructive (10)
Deceiving (8)
Diverted; taken away; also charmed or delighted (8)
Eagerness; quickness (8)
Earnestly request (7)
Farm; granary (6)
Fawning; showing servile compliance (10)
Fed to excess (9)
Gullible (9)
Having lost courage (8)
Implying; introducing an idea subtlely (11)
Induced to commit a bad action or perjury (8)
Intelligence; humor (3)
Officially announce (10)
Promotion (10)
Puffed-up; pompous (7)
Repeated requests (11)
Reward; indulge; satisfy (7)
Secretly plot (8)
Sin(s) (8)
Something in the way; a hindrance (10)
Something of little importance or value (6)
Soon (4)
Spite; ill-will (6)
To be slow in leaving (6)
Total ruin; damnation (9)
Uncontrolled; unrestrained (11)
Used to express distaste or disapproval (3)
Violent storm (7)
Vulgar; humorously coarse (5)

Othello Vocabulary Word Search 3

Words are placed backwards, forward, diagonally, up and down. Words listed below are included in the maze. Circle the hidden vocabulary words in the maze.

```
B K P Q F M A N D A T E H I I P I C F
L A S C I V I O U S R C C N M R N R W
W D W D E B Q T N I A A I C V O S E W
C K V D N H S B P O S Q L O X M I D M
S N J R Y A L S R T U V I N K U N U R
S T P X B T N P I I V S N T E L U L E
R X B M T O E G T M M U G I X G A O G
P E O E C R A Y R Q P B E N P A T U R
R B Q W S T G W Z J B O R E O T I S E
E D W U I E D G O S V R R N S E N X G
F L H O I C E Y C O V N M T Q G E I
E G N N L S N C G C E E B A U A G Z O
R X C F S R I K H Q J D W P L N R N U
M V P R A H C T C L E M S A A I I Y S
E Y F I T A R G E L Y A C R T G C T L
N E L F I R T I U S J R G S E Q V E Y
T E M P E S T D F D I S M A Y E D W L
W B Q D T Q I M P T P E R D I T I O N
G H S J Y N C W Y I B E G U I L E D K
C Z D Q G A N O N W P E R I L B A S E
```

ALACRITY	DELUDING	INSINUATING	REPROACH
ANON	DISMAYED	LASCIVIOUS	REQUISITES
BASE	EGREGIOUSLY	LINGER	SATIETY
BAWDY	EXPOSTULATE	MALICE	SHRIFT
BEGUILED	FIE	MANDATE	SUBORNED
BESEECH	GRANGE	MARS	TEMPEST
BOMBAST	GRATIFY	PERDITION	TRIFLE
CASTIGATION	IMPORTUNITY	PERIL	WIT
CONSPIRE	INCONTINENT	PREFERMENT	WOOED
CREDULOUS	INIQUITY	PROMULGATE	

Othello Vocabulary Word Search 3 Answer Key

Words are placed backwards, forward, diagonally, up and down. Words listed below are included in the maze. Circle the hidden vocabulary words in the maze.

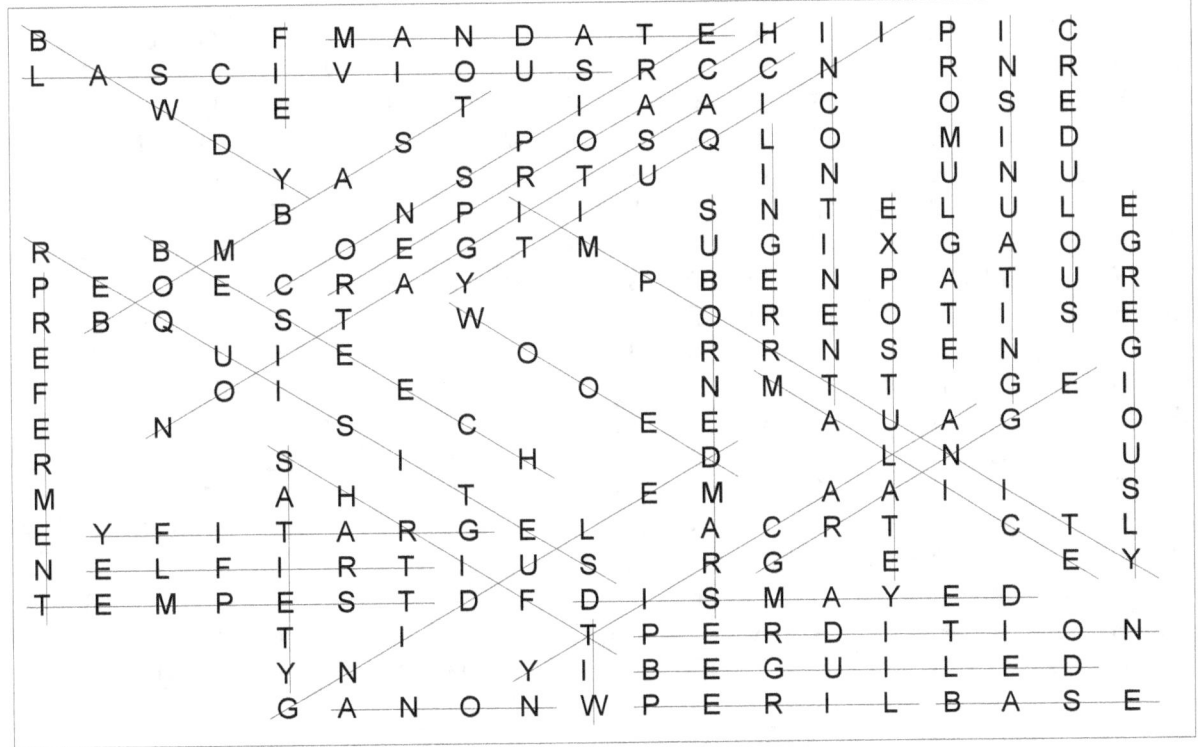

ALACRITY	DELUDING	INSINUATING	REPROACH
ANON	DISMAYED	LASCIVIOUS	REQUISITES
BASE	EGREGIOUSLY	LINGER	SATIETY
BAWDY	EXPOSTULATE	MALICE	SHRIFT
BEGUILED	FIE	MANDATE	SUBORNED
BESEECH	GRANGE	MARS	TEMPEST
BOMBAST	GRATIFY	PERDITION	TRIFLE
CASTIGATION	IMPORTUNITY	PERIL	WIT
CONSPIRE	INCONTINENT	PREFERMENT	WOOED
CREDULOUS	INIQUITY	PROMULGATE	

Othello Vocabulary Word Search 4

Words are placed backwards, forward, diagonally, up and down. Words listed below are included in the maze. Circle the hidden vocabulary words in the maze.

```
V W F T K J A T S B L W E R Z M D B G
T F I R H S Y L S U O I G E R G E E R
N V N I C R F G A O F M N B Y L L G L
Z V N F E A P M E C R M B G J P U U R
Q P P L E M K D L H R W A A E W D I C
T R R E S A T I E T Y I W N S R I L X
N E O I E G R H N M A C T W D T N E D
E F M M B E B W D S D N Y Y E A G D E
M E U P P B N N E W I T O C S G T G B
I R L O E L O R N B S N I N A C N E N
D M G R M S I E R B M L U Q B A E B H
E E A T R P T Q O Y A S R A R N N A C
P N T U S V A U B M Y U E G T O I W Z
M T E N F M C I U T E R P R B I T D Y
I N O I K W O S S C D F R A Q T N Y W
R C Z T B G V I J W Q E O T R I O G J
N T S Y M P D T T R Z I A I L D C V B
J B Q V B R A E K W Q T C F J R N Y P
S U O I U Q E S B O P E H Y R E I F D
P E R N I C I O U S J D C D Z P R R Q
```

ADVOCATION	DISMAYED	MALICE	REQUISITES
ALACRITY	EGREGIOUSLY	MANDATE	SATIETY
ANON	FIE	MARS	SHRIFT
BASE	GRANGE	OBSEQUIOUS	SUBORNED
BAWDY	GRATIFY	PERDITION	SURFEITED
BEGUILED	IMPEDIMENT	PERIL	TEMPEST
BESEECH	IMPORTUNITY	PERNICIOUS	TRIFLE
BOMBAST	INCONTINENT	PREFERMENT	WIT
CONSPIRE	INSINUATING	PROMULGATE	WOOED
DELUDING	LINGER	REPROACH	

Othello Vocabulary Word Search 4 Answer Key

Words are placed backwards, forward, diagonally, up and down. Words listed below are included in the maze. Circle the hidden vocabulary words in the maze.

ADVOCATION	DISMAYED	MALICE	REQUISITES
ALACRITY	EGREGIOUSLY	MANDATE	SATIETY
ANON	FIE	MARS	SHRIFT
BASE	GRANGE	OBSEQUIOUS	SUBORNED
BAWDY	GRATIFY	PERDITION	SURFEITED
BEGUILED	IMPEDIMENT	PERIL	TEMPEST
BESEECH	IMPORTUNITY	PERNICIOUS	TRIFLE
BOMBAST	INCONTINENT	PREFERMENT	WIT
CONSPIRE	INSINUATING	PROMULGATE	WOOED
DELUDING	LINGER	REPROACH	

Othello Vocabulary Crossword 1

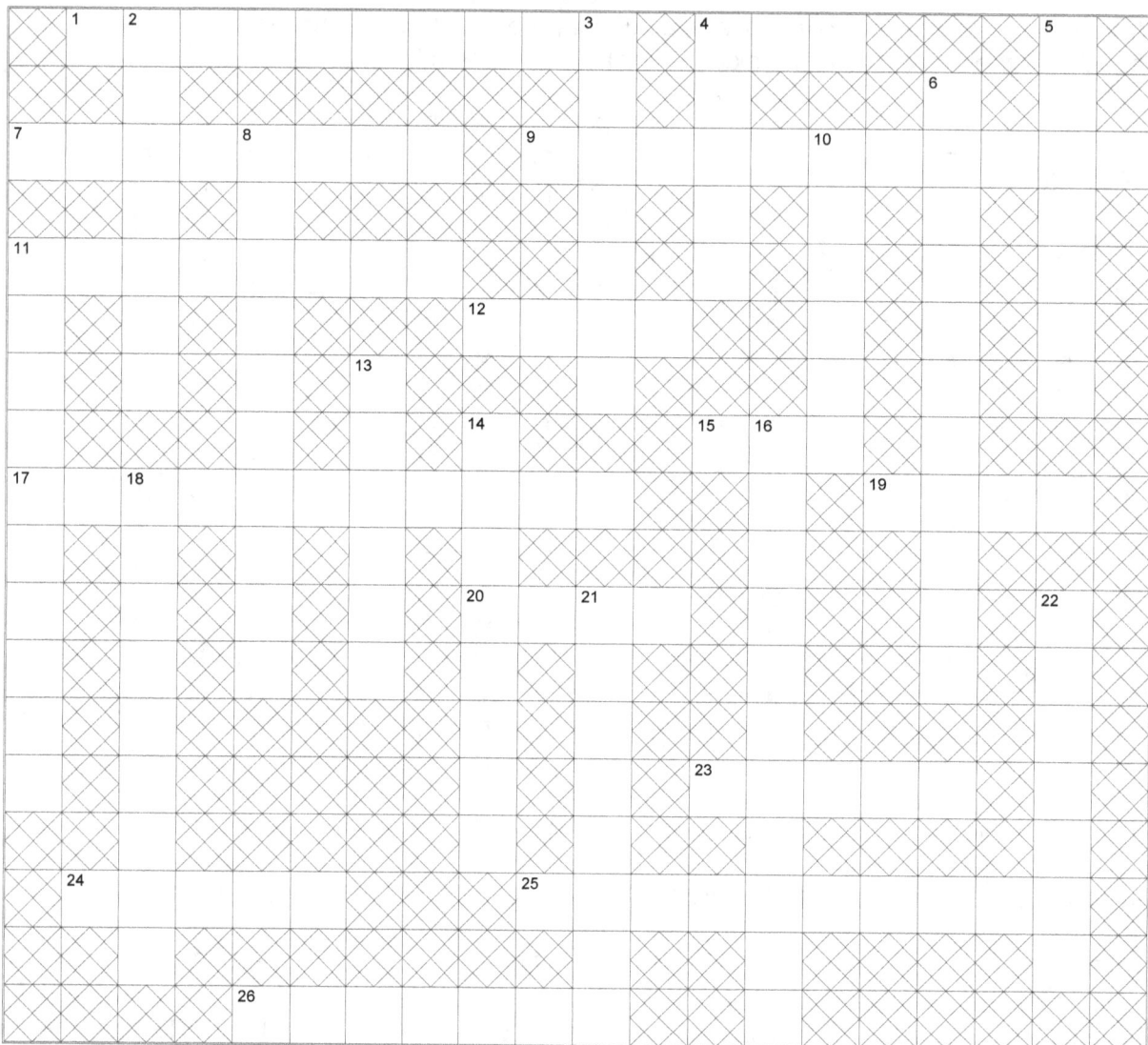

Across
1. Something in the way; a hindrance
4. Intelligence; humor
7. Secretly plot
9. Repeated requests
11. Eagerness; quickness
12. Common; low in station
15. Used to express distaste or disapproval
17. Punishment; criticism
19. Soon
20. Damages; marks
23. Vulgar; humorously coarse
24. Danger
25. Lecherous
26. Earnestly request

Down
2. Command; official instruction
3. Violent storm
4. Courted; dated
5. Condition of being over-filled or over-gratified
6. Uncontrolled; unrestrained
8. Deadly; destructive
10. Something of little importance or value
11. A cause; a path of action
13. Farm; granary
14. Having lost courage
16. Implying; introducing an idea subtlely
18. Fed to excess
21. Criticism; disgrace; blame; shame
22. Puffed-up; pompous

Othello Vocabulary Crossword 1 Answer Key

Across
1. Something in the way; a hindrance
4. Intelligence; humor
7. Secretly plot
9. Repeated requests
11. Eagerness; quickness
12. Common; low in station
15. Used to express distaste or disapproval
17. Punishment; criticism
19. Soon
20. Damages; marks
23. Vulgar; humorously coarse
24. Danger
25. Lecherous
26. Earnestly request

Down
2. Command; official instruction
3. Violent storm
4. Courted; dated
5. Condition of being over-filled or over-gratified
6. Uncontrolled; unrestrained
8. Deadly; destructive
10. Something of little importance or value
11. A cause; a path of action
13. Farm; granary
14. Having lost courage
16. Implying; introducing an idea subtlely
18. Fed to excess
21. Criticism; disgrace; blame; shame
22. Puffed-up; pompous

Othello Vocabulary Crossword 2

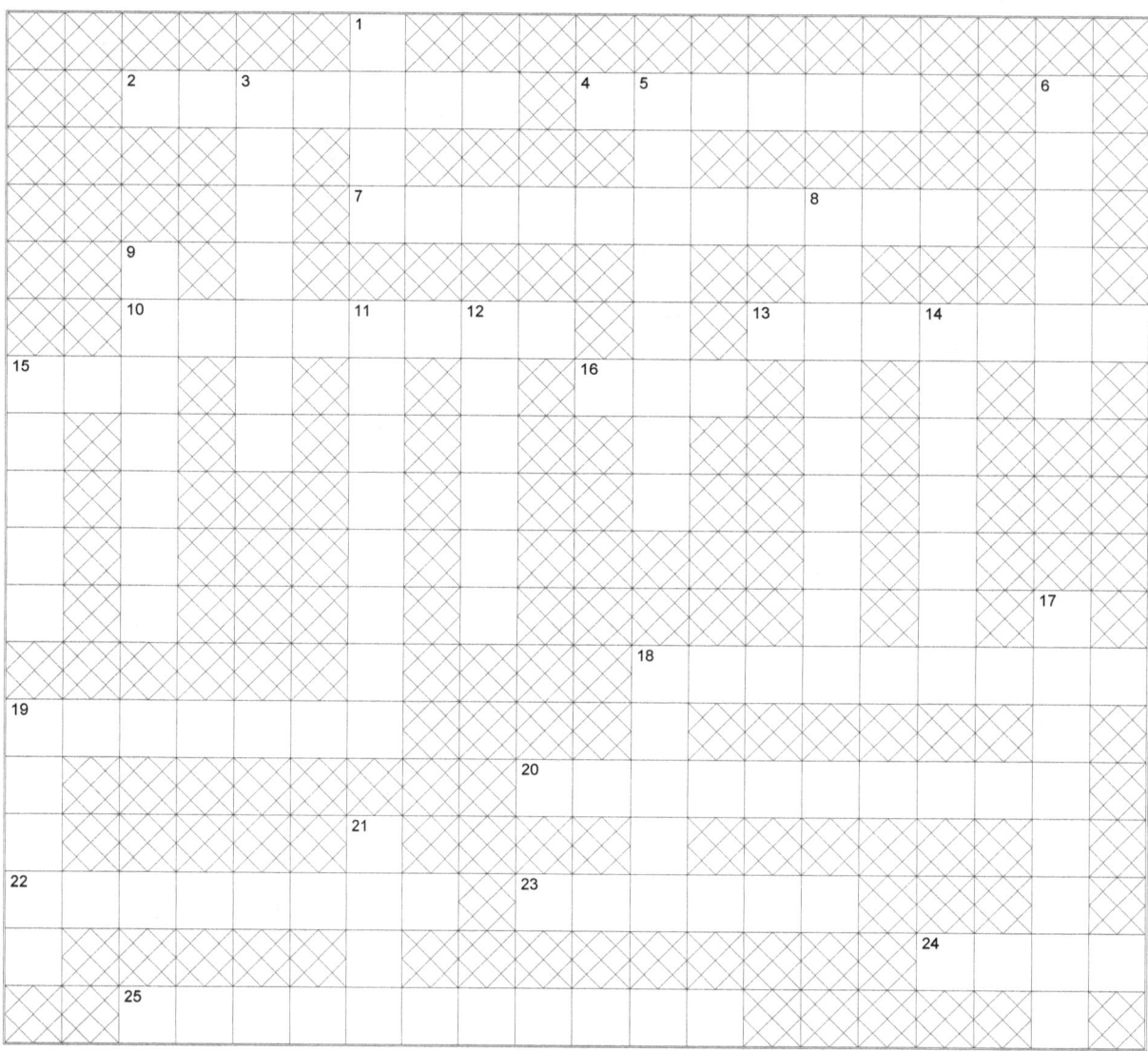

Across
2. Puffed-up; pompous
4. To be slow in leaving
7. Conspicuously offensively
10. Eagerness; quickness
13. Reward; indulge; satisfy
15. Intelligence; humor
16. Used to express distaste or disapproval
18. Total ruin; damnation
19. Earnestly request
20. Deadly; destructive
22. Deceiving
23. Spite; ill-will
24. Damages; marks
25. Uncontrolled; unrestrained

Down
1. Common; low in station
3. Command; official instruction
5. Sin(s)
6. Confessional
8. Fed to excess
9. Condition of being over-filled or over-gratified
11. Criticism; disgrace; blame; shame
12. Something of little importance or value
14. Violent storm
15. Courted; dated
17. Secretly plot
18. Danger
19. Vulgar; humorously coarse
21. Soon

Othello Vocabulary Crossword 2 Answer Key

```
            1 B
      2 B O M B A S T         4 L  5 I N G E R            6 S
            A   S                    N                     H
            N   7 E G R E G I O U S  8 L Y                 R
        9 S D                        Q    U                I
          10 A L A C R 11 I 12 T Y  13 U G R A 14 T I F Y
   15 W  I T    T     E    R    16 F I E    F    E    T
   O    I      E     P    I       T       E    M
   O    E      R     F              Y         I    P
   E    T      O     L                        T    E
   D    Y      A     E                        E  17 C
                 C                18 P E R D  I  T  I  O  N
19 B E S E E C H                    E                     N
 A                           20 P E R N I C I O U S
 W                           21 A                          P
22 D E L U D I N G         23 M A L I C E
 Y                                              24 M A R S
              25 I N C O N T I N E N T              E
```

Across
2. Puffed-up; pompous
4. To be slow in leaving
7. Conspicuously offensively
10. Eagerness; quickness
13. Reward; indulge; satisfy
15. Intelligence; humor
16. Used to express distaste or disapproval
18. Total ruin; damnation
19. Earnestly request
20. Deadly; destructive
22. Deceiving
23. Spite; ill-will
24. Damages; marks
25. Uncontrolled; unrestrained

Down
1. Common; low in station
3. Command; official instruction
5. Sin(s)
6. Confessional
8. Fed to excess
9. Condition of being over-filled or over-gratified
11. Criticism; disgrace; blame; shame
12. Something of little importance or value
14. Violent storm
15. Courted; dated
17. Secretly plot
18. Danger
19. Vulgar; humorously coarse
21. Soon

Othello Vocabulary Crossword 3

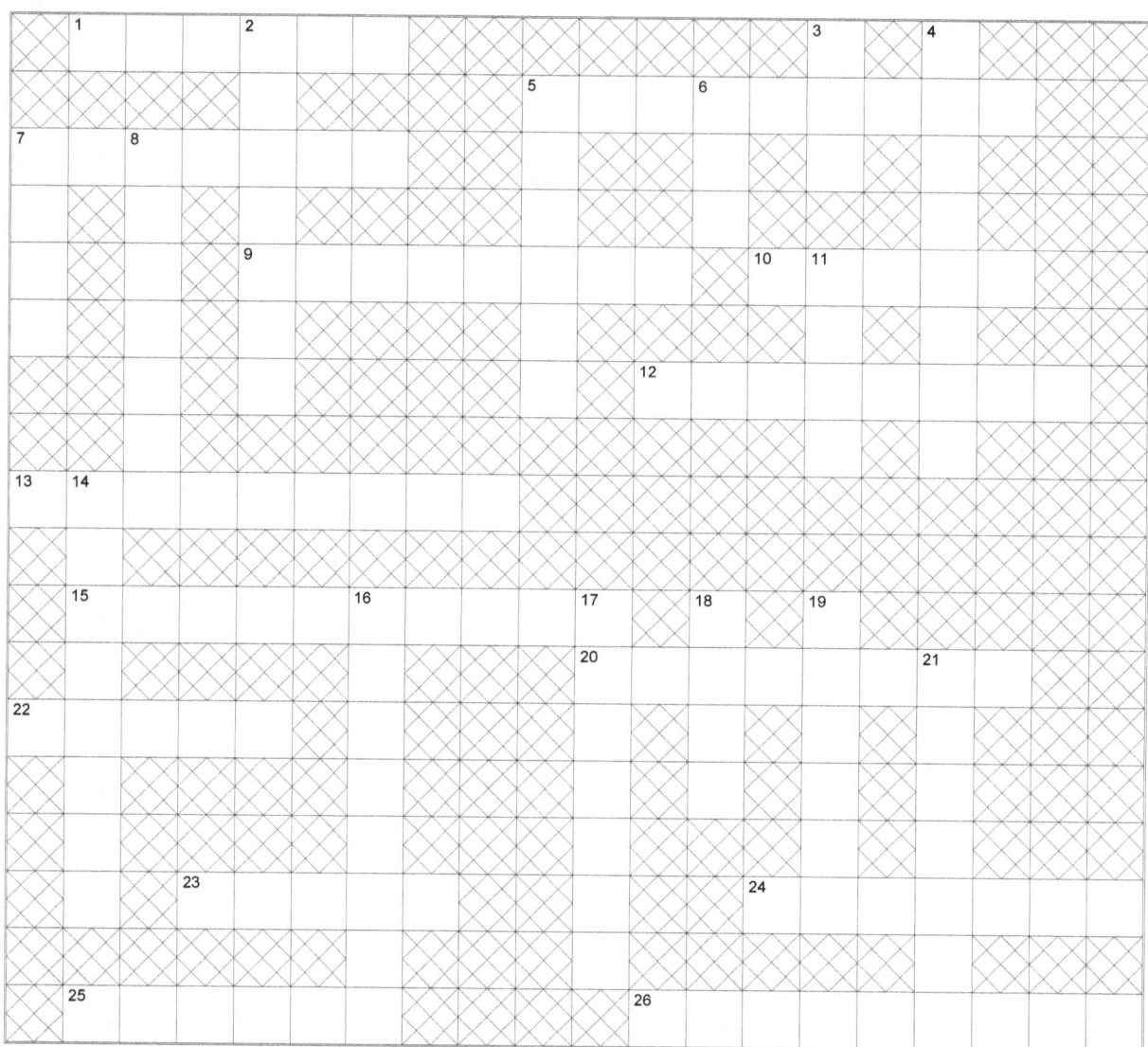

Across
1. To be slow in leaving
5. Fed to excess
7. Puffed-up; pompous
9. Sin(s)
10. Vulgar; humorously coarse
12. Induced to commit a bad action or perjury
13. Gullible
15. Deadly; destructive
20. Eagerness; quickness
22. Courted; dated
23. Danger
24. Earnestly request
25. Farm; granary
26. Total ruin; damnation

Down
2. Reward; indulge; satisfy
3. Intelligence; humor
4. Deceiving
5. Confessional
6. Used to express distaste or disapproval
7. Common; low in station
8. Command; official instruction
11. Soon
14. Criticism; disgrace; blame; shame
16. Secretly plot
17. Condition of being over-filled or over-gratified
18. Damages; marks
19. Something of little importance or value
21. Violent storm

Othello Vocabulary Crossword 3 Answer Key

Across
1. To be slow in leaving
5. Fed to excess
7. Puffed-up; pompous
9. Sin(s)
10. Vulgar; humorously coarse
12. Induced to commit a bad action or perjury
13. Gullible
15. Deadly; destructive
20. Eagerness; quickness
22. Courted; dated
23. Danger
24. Earnestly request
25. Farm; granary
26. Total ruin; damnation

Down
2. Reward; indulge; satisfy
3. Intelligence; humor
4. Deceiving
5. Confessional
6. Used to express distaste or disapproval
7. Common; low in station
8. Command; official instruction
11. Soon
14. Criticism; disgrace; blame; shame
16. Secretly plot
17. Condition of being over-filled or over-gratified
18. Damages; marks
19. Something of little importance or value
21. Violent storm

Othello Vocabulary Crossword 4

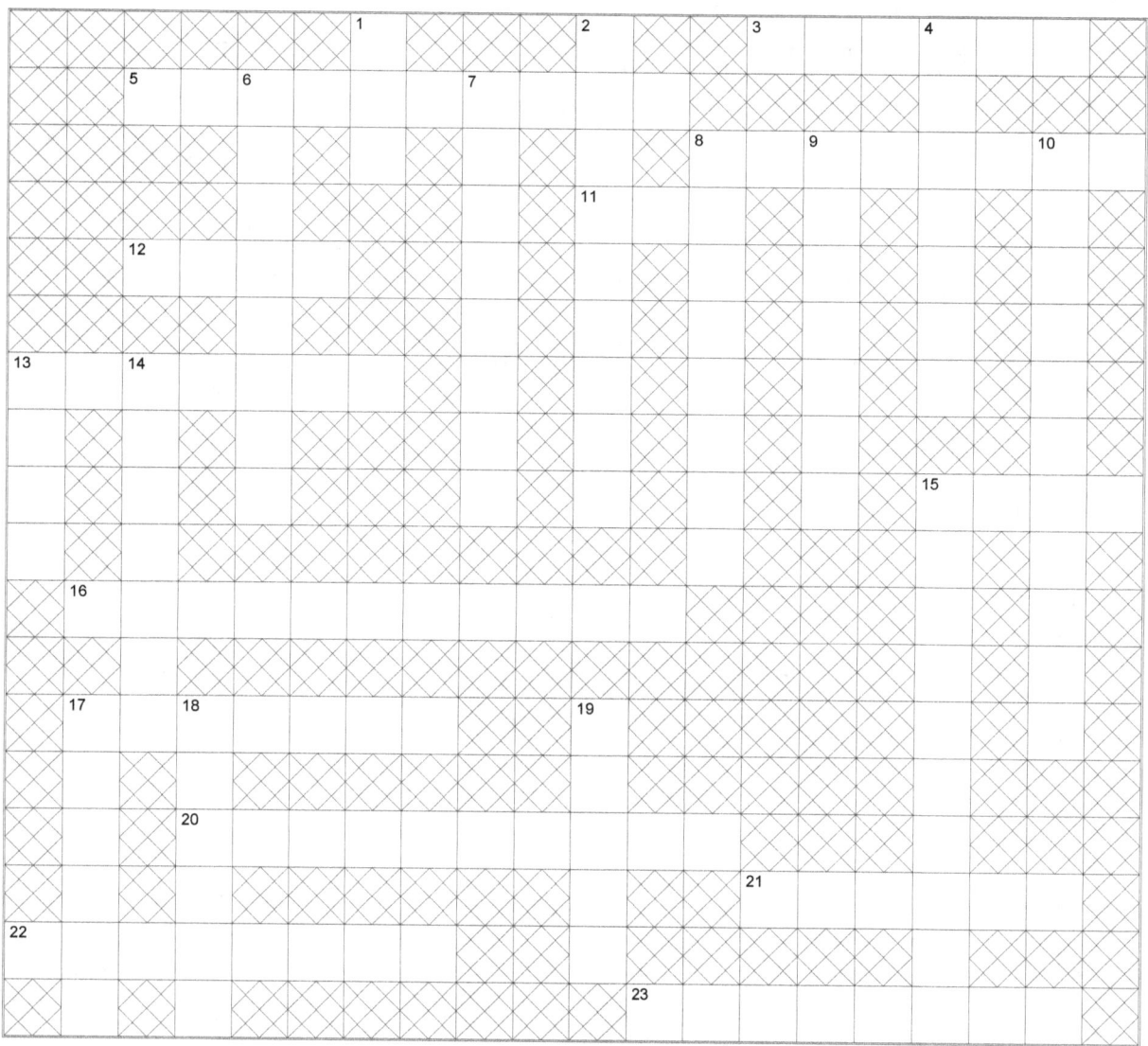

Across
- 3. To be slow in leaving
- 5. Deadly; destructive
- 8. Having lost courage
- 11. Used to express distaste or disapproval
- 12. Damages; marks
- 13. Puffed-up; pompous
- 15. Soon
- 16. Punishment; criticism
- 17. Violent storm
- 20. Lecherous
- 21. Confessional
- 22. Eagerness; quickness
- 23. Induced to commit a bad action or perjury

Down
- 1. Intelligence; humor
- 2. Fed to excess
- 4. Reward; indulge; satisfy
- 6. Criticism; disgrace; blame; shame
- 7. Sin(s)
- 8. Deceiving
- 9. Condition of being over-filled or over-gratified
- 10. Conspicuously offensively
- 13. Common; low in station
- 14. Command; official instruction
- 15. A cause; a path of action
- 17. Something of little importance or value
- 18. Spite; ill-will
- 19. Courted; dated

Othello Vocabulary Crossword 4 Answer Key

				¹W				²S			³L	I	N	⁴G	E	R
	⁵P	E	⁶R	N	I	⁷C	I	O	U	S				R		
			E		T		N		R		⁸D	I	⁹S	M	A	Y	E	D
			P				I		¹¹F	I	E		M		A		¹⁰T		G
		¹²M	A	R	S		Q		E		L		T		I		F		R
			O				U		I		U		I		F		E
¹³B	O	¹⁴M	B	A	S	T		I		T		D		E		T		Y		G
A		A		C				T		E		I		T				¹⁵A	N	O	N
S		N		H				Y		D		N		Y		D		U
E		D										G				V		S
	¹⁶C	A	S	T	I	G	A	T	I	O	N				O		L
		T													C		Y
	¹⁷T	E	¹⁸M	P	E	S	T		¹⁹W				C		Y
	R		A						O				A
	I		²⁰L	A	S	C	I	V	I	O	U	S		T
	F		I						E		²¹S	H	R	I	F	T
²²A	L	A	C	R	I	T	Y		D				O
	E		E						²³S	U	B	O	R	N	E	D

Across
3. To be slow in leaving
5. Deadly; destructive
8. Having lost courage
11. Used to express distaste or disapproval
12. Damages; marks
13. Puffed-up; pompous
15. Soon
16. Punishment; criticism
17. Violent storm
20. Lecherous
21. Confessional
22. Eagerness; quickness
23. Induced to commit a bad action or perjury

Down
1. Intelligence; humor
2. Fed to excess
4. Reward; indulge; satisfy
6. Criticism; disgrace; blame; shame
7. Sin(s)
8. Deceiving
9. Condition of being over-filled or over-gratified
10. Conspicuously offensively
13. Common; low in station
14. Command; official instruction
15. A cause; a path of action
17. Something of little importance or value
18. Spite; ill-will
19. Courted; dated

Othello Vocabulary Juggle Letters 1

1. NONA = 1. _____
   Soon

2. OVDAOACNIT = 2. _____
   A cause; a path of action

3. PRCRAEOH = 3. _____
   Criticism; disgrace; blame; shame

4. MCAELI = 4. _____
   Spite; ill-will

5. OOEWD = 5. _____
   Courted; dated

6. DINPMMITEE = 6. _____
   Something in the way; a hindrance

7. LERTIF = 7. _____
   Something of little importance or value

8. FRTGAYI = 8. _____
   Reward; indulge; satisfy

9. OSRUDCLEU = 9. _____
   Gullible

10. EIFDTSEUR =10. _____
    Fed to excess

11. LACRTIAY =11. _____
    Eagerness; quickness

12. BOBMAST =12. _____
    Puffed-up; pompous

13. IEF =13. _____
    Used to express distaste or disapproval

14. ERPUSONICI =14. _____
    Deadly; destructive

15. QUOBSOUSEI =15. _____
    Fawning; showing servile compliance

Othello Vocabulary Juggle Letters 1 Answer Key

1. NONA = 1. ANON
   Soon

2. OVDAOACNIT = 2. ADVOCATION
   A cause; a path of action

3. PRCRAEOH = 3. REPROACH
   Criticism; disgrace; blame; shame

4. MCAELI = 4. MALICE
   Spite; ill-will

5. OOEWD = 5. WOOED
   Courted; dated

6. DINPMMITEE = 6. IMPEDIMENT
   Something in the way; a hindrance

7. LERTIF = 7. TRIFLE
   Something of little importance or value

8. FRTGAYI = 8. GRATIFY
   Reward; indulge; satisfy

9. OSRUDCLEU = 9. CREDULOUS
   Gullible

10. EIFDTSEUR = 10. SURFEITED
    Fed to excess

11. LACRTIAY = 11. ALACRITY
    Eagerness; quickness

12. BOBMAST = 12. BOMBAST
    Puffed-up; pompous

13. IEF = 13. FIE
    Used to express distaste or disapproval

14. ERPUSONICI = 14. PERNICIOUS
    Deadly; destructive

15. QUOBSOUSEI = 15. OBSEQUIOUS
    Fawning; showing servile compliance

Othello Vocabulary Juggle Letters 2

1. ODEOW = 1. _____
   Courted; dated

2. CNISIOPURE = 2. _____
   Deadly; destructive

3. GDENUIDL = 3. _____
   Deceiving

4. GGILSERYOUE = 4. _____
   Conspicuously offensively

5. GILDBUEE = 5. _____
   Diverted; taken away; also charmed or delighted

6. QUIOUOSBSE = 6. _____
   Fawning; showing servile compliance

7. EGNIRL = 7. _____
   To be slow in leaving

8. ECEEHBS = 8. _____
   Earnestly request

9. ILAISUOCVS = 9. _____
   Lecherous

10. TTYSIAE = 10. _____
    Condition of being over-filled or over-gratified

11. NOITIDRPE = 11. _____
    Total ruin; damnation

12. RLCYAATI = 12. _____
    Eagerness; quickness

13. INOEPSRC = 13. _____
    Secretly plot

14. SQTUESERII = 14. _____
    Requirements

15. PUEESTAXOTL = 15. _____
    Reason earnestly

Othello Vocabulary Juggle Letters 2 Answer Key

1. ODEOW = 1. WOOED
   Courted; dated

2. CNISIOPURE = 2. PERNICIOUS
   Deadly; destructive

3. GDENUIDL = 3. DELUDING
   Deceiving

4. GGILSERYOUE = 4. EGREGIOUSLY
   Conspicuously offensively

5. GILDBUEE = 5. BEGUILED
   Diverted; taken away; also charmed or delighted

6. QUIOUOSBSE = 6. OBSEQUIOUS
   Fawning; showing servile compliance

7. EGNIRL = 7. LINGER
   To be slow in leaving

8. ECEEHBS = 8. BESEECH
   Earnestly request

9. ILAISUOCVS = 9. LASCIVIOUS
   Lecherous

10. TTYSIAE = 10. SATIETY
    Condition of being over-filled or over-gratified

11. NOITIDRPE = 11. PERDITION
    Total ruin; damnation

12. RLCYAATI = 12. ALACRITY
    Eagerness; quickness

13. INOEPSRC = 13. CONSPIRE
    Secretly plot

14. SQTUESERII = 14. REQUISITES
    Requirements

15. PUEESTAXOTL = 15. EXPOSTULATE
    Reason earnestly

Othello Vocabulary Juggle Letters 3

1. YITINUIQ = 1. _____
   Sin(s)

2. LIMACE = 2. _____
   Spite; ill-will

3. EIONPRDIT = 3. _____
   Total ruin; damnation

4. EIRFTL = 4. _____
   Something of little importance or value

5. TGAELOURMP = 5. _____
   Officially announce

6. IDEEFSTUR = 6. _____
   Fed to excess

7. ROPIYTUITNM = 7. _____
   Repeated requests

8. SIOSOBEQUU = 8. _____
   Fawning; showing servile compliance

9. AOMBSBT = 9. _____
   Puffed-up; pompous

10. EABS =10. _____
    Common; low in station

11. REIPL =11. _____
    Danger

12. XAEPLSOUETT =12. _____
    Reason earnestly

13. NRGLEI =13. _____
    To be slow in leaving

14. LEUIEGBD =14. _____
    Diverted; taken away; also charmed or delighted

15. TYEIAST =15. _____
    Condition of being over-filled or over-gratified

Othello Vocabulary Juggle Letters 3 Answer Key

1. YITINUIQ = 1. INIQUITY
   Sin(s)

2. LIMACE = 2. MALICE
   Spite; ill-will

3. EIONPRDIT = 3. PERDITION
   Total ruin; damnation

4. EIRFTL = 4. TRIFLE
   Something of little importance or value

5. TGAELOURMP = 5. PROMULGATE
   Officially announce

6. IDEEFSTUR = 6. SURFEITED
   Fed to excess

7. ROPIYTUITNM = 7. IMPORTUNITY
   Repeated requests

8. SIOSOBEQUU = 8. OBSEQUIOUS
   Fawning; showing servile compliance

9. AOMBSBT = 9. BOMBAST
   Puffed-up; pompous

10. EABS = 10. BASE
    Common; low in station

11. REIPL = 11. PERIL
    Danger

12. XAEPLSOUETT = 12. EXPOSTULATE
    Reason earnestly

13. NRGLEI = 13. LINGER
    To be slow in leaving

14. LEUIEGBD = 14. BEGUILED
    Diverted; taken away; also charmed or delighted

15. TYEIAST = 15. SATIETY
    Condition of being over-filled or over-gratified

Othello Vocabulary Juggle Letters 4

1. TASIEYT = 1. _____
   Condition of being over-filled or over-gratified

2. YUSIEGERGOL = 2. _____
   Conspicuously offensively

3. RPTNFEMEER = 3. _____
   Promotion

4. RYIAGTF = 4. _____
   Reward; indulge; satisfy

5. NOAN = 5. _____
   Soon

6. MBSBTAO = 6. _____
   Puffed-up; pompous

7. RNEAGG = 7. _____
   Farm; granary

8. OOEWD = 8. _____
   Courted; dated

9. ICNNTTONIEN = 9. _____
   Uncontrolled; unrestrained

10. IMEIDTNEPM =10. _____
    Something in the way; a hindrance

11. IEASDMYD =11. _____
    Having lost courage

12. YWABD =12. _____
    Vulgar; humorously coarse

13. UTIIQINY =13. _____
    Sin(s)

14. NEDTMAA =14. _____
    Command; official instruction

15. IFE =15. _____
    Used to express distaste or disapproval

Othello Vocabulary Juggle Letters 4 Answer Key

1. TASIEYT = 1. SATIETY
   Condition of being over-filled or over-gratified

2. YUSIEGERGOL = 2. EGREGIOUSLY
   Conspicuously offensively

3. RPTNFEMEER = 3. PREFERMENT
   Promotion

4. RYIAGTF = 4. GRATIFY
   Reward; indulge; satisfy

5. NOAN = 5. ANON
   Soon

6. MBSBTAO = 6. BOMBAST
   Puffed-up; pompous

7. RNEAGG = 7. GRANGE
   Farm; granary

8. OOEWD = 8. WOOED
   Courted; dated

9. ICNNTTONIEN = 9. INCONTINENT
   Uncontrolled; unrestrained

10. IMEIDTNEPM = 10. IMPEDIMENT
    Something in the way; a hindrance

11. IEASDMYD = 11. DISMAYED
    Having lost courage

12. YWABD = 12. BAWDY
    Vulgar; humorously coarse

13. UTIIQINY = 13. INIQUITY
    Sin(s)

14. NEDTMAA = 14. MANDATE
    Command; official instruction

15. IFE = 15. FIE
    Used to express distaste or disapproval

ADVOCATION	A cause; a path of action
ALACRITY	Eagerness; quickness
ANON	Soon
BASE	Common; low in station
BAWDY	Vulgar; humorously coarse
BEGUILED	Diverted; taken away; also charmed or delighted

BESEECH	Earnestly request
BOMBAST	Puffed-up; pompous
CASTIGATION	Punishment; criticism
CONSPIRE	Secretly plot
CREDULOUS	Gullible
DELUDING	Deceiving

DISMAYED	Having lost courage
EGREGIOUSLY	Conspicuously offensively
EXPOSTULATE	Reason earnestly
FIE	Used to express distaste or disapproval
GRANGE	Farm; granary
GRATIFY	Reward; indulge; satisfy

IMPEDIMENT	Something in the way; a hindrance
IMPORTUNITY	Repeated requests
INCONTINENT	Uncontrolled; unrestrained
INIQUITY	Sin(s)
INSINUATING	Implying; introducing an idea subtlely
LASCIVIOUS	Lecherous

LINGER	To be slow in leaving
MALICE	Spite; ill-will
MANDATE	Command; official instruction
MARS	Damages; marks
OBSEQUIOUS	Fawning; showing servile compliance
PERDITION	Total ruin; damnation

PERIL	Danger
PERNICIOUS	Deadly; destructive
PREFERMENT	Promotion
PROMULGATE	Officially announce
REPROACH	Criticism; disgrace; blame; shame
REQUISITES	Requirements

SATIETY	Condition of being over-filled or over-gratified
SHRIFT	Confessional
SUBORNED	Induced to commit a bad action or perjury
SURFEITED	Fed to excess
TEMPEST	Violent storm
TRIFLE	Something of little importance or value

WIT	Intelligence; humor
WOOED	Courted; dated

Othello Vocabulary

WOOED	SATIETY	TEMPEST	MARS	PREFERMENT
SUBORNED	SURFEITED	INCONTINENT	INSINUATING	BASE
IMPORTUNITY	CREDULOUS	FREE SPACE	PERNICIOUS	FIE
CASTIGATION	PERIL	ANON	REQUISITES	DELUDING
BOMBAST	LINGER	CONSPIRE	IMPEDIMENT	ALACRITY

Othello Vocabulary

BESEECH	PROMULGATE	EXPOSTULATE	DISMAYED	GRATIFY
BEGUILED	TRIFLE	ADVOCATION	INIQUITY	GRANGE
OBSEQUIOUS	SHRIFT	FREE SPACE	LASCIVIOUS	EGREGIOUSLY
MANDATE	MALICE	WIT	PERDITION	ALACRITY
IMPEDIMENT	CONSPIRE	LINGER	BOMBAST	DELUDING

Othello Vocabulary

INSINUATING	SHRIFT	SATIETY	PERNICIOUS	ALACRITY
CONSPIRE	PROMULGATE	BAWDY	BESEECH	SURFEITED
LINGER	GRANGE	FREE SPACE	ANON	BEGUILED
BASE	OBSEQUIOUS	LASCIVIOUS	BOMBAST	INIQUITY
DISMAYED	GRATIFY	IMPEDIMENT	WIT	WOOED

Othello Vocabulary

FIE	ADVOCATION	PERIL	SUBORNED	TEMPEST
CASTIGATION	EGREGIOUSLY	CREDULOUS	IMPORTUNITY	MALICE
TRIFLE	PREFERMENT	FREE SPACE	REQUISITES	INCONTINENT
PERDITION	EXPOSTULATE	DELUDING	REPROACH	WOOED
WIT	IMPEDIMENT	GRATIFY	DISMAYED	INIQUITY

Othello Vocabulary

EXPOSTULATE	WIT	INIQUITY	PERNICIOUS	MARS
FIE	GRANGE	SATIETY	INCONTINENT	INSINUATING
IMPEDIMENT	LASCIVIOUS	FREE SPACE	ANON	BEGUILED
TRIFLE	MALICE	WOOED	CONSPIRE	SHRIFT
ADVOCATION	MANDATE	GRATIFY	PROMULGATE	SUBORNED

Othello Vocabulary

EGREGIOUSLY	PERDITION	PREFERMENT	REPROACH	IMPORTUNITY
ALACRITY	BAWDY	DELUDING	SURFEITED	BASE
CASTIGATION	LINGER	FREE SPACE	BESEECH	REQUISITES
CREDULOUS	PERIL	BOMBAST	TEMPEST	SUBORNED
PROMULGATE	GRATIFY	MANDATE	ADVOCATION	SHRIFT

Othello Vocabulary

SATIETY	GRATIFY	IMPORTUNITY	PERDITION	LINGER
INCONTINENT	FIE	MANDATE	BEGUILED	TRIFLE
SURFEITED	WIT	FREE SPACE	ADVOCATION	EGREGIOUSLY
BAWDY	CREDULOUS	PERIL	BESEECH	SHRIFT
DELUDING	MARS	PREFERMENT	MALICE	DISMAYED

Othello Vocabulary

PERNICIOUS	PROMULGATE	TEMPEST	GRANGE	SUBORNED
REPROACH	IMPEDIMENT	ANON	CASTIGATION	CONSPIRE
REQUISITES	BOMBAST	FREE SPACE	OBSEQUIOUS	ALACRITY
BASE	INSINUATING	INIQUITY	EXPOSTULATE	DISMAYED
MALICE	PREFERMENT	MARS	DELUDING	SHRIFT

Othello Vocabulary

BASE	TRIFLE	BEGUILED	SURFEITED	BESEECH
REQUISITES	ANON	FIE	WOOED	WIT
PREFERMENT	IMPEDIMENT	FREE SPACE	DELUDING	PERDITION
EXPOSTULATE	DISMAYED	SATIETY	LASCIVIOUS	INSINUATING
MARS	PROMULGATE	TEMPEST	MANDATE	OBSEQUIOUS

Othello Vocabulary

CASTIGATION	ALACRITY	SHRIFT	MALICE	INIQUITY
EGREGIOUSLY	CONSPIRE	IMPORTUNITY	GRANGE	PERIL
GRATIFY	SUBORNED	FREE SPACE	INCONTINENT	BAWDY
PERNICIOUS	CREDULOUS	REPROACH	LINGER	OBSEQUIOUS
MANDATE	TEMPEST	PROMULGATE	MARS	INSINUATING

Othello Vocabulary

WOOED	DELUDING	IMPEDIMENT	PERDITION	INSINUATING
IMPORTUNITY	CONSPIRE	TRIFLE	WIT	PERIL
REQUISITES	ANON	FREE SPACE	GRANGE	TEMPEST
CREDULOUS	PROMULGATE	OBSEQUIOUS	LASCIVIOUS	SATIETY
MARS	BOMBAST	BESEECH	EXPOSTULATE	LINGER

Othello Vocabulary

INIQUITY	BAWDY	EGREGIOUSLY	SUBORNED	GRATIFY
DISMAYED	PREFERMENT	SURFEITED	REPROACH	PERNICIOUS
MALICE	SHRIFT	FREE SPACE	CASTIGATION	INCONTINENT
BASE	ADVOCATION	MANDATE	ALACRITY	LINGER
EXPOSTULATE	BESEECH	BOMBAST	MARS	SATIETY

Othello Vocabulary

INCONTINENT	PERIL	FIE	GRANGE	BASE
ADVOCATION	LASCIVIOUS	BAWDY	CASTIGATION	SATIETY
SURFEITED	WOOED	FREE SPACE	REPROACH	WIT
PERNICIOUS	MANDATE	GRATIFY	TEMPEST	EGREGIOUSLY
CREDULOUS	BEGUILED	ALACRITY	SUBORNED	OBSEQUIOUS

Othello Vocabulary

EXPOSTULATE	BESEECH	MARS	PREFERMENT	MALICE
PERDITION	IMPORTUNITY	CONSPIRE	ANON	INIQUITY
IMPEDIMENT	DISMAYED	FREE SPACE	INSINUATING	REQUISITES
TRIFLE	BOMBAST	SHRIFT	DELUDING	OBSEQUIOUS
SUBORNED	ALACRITY	BEGUILED	CREDULOUS	EGREGIOUSLY

Othello Vocabulary

BESEECH	PERNICIOUS	WIT	IMPORTUNITY	PERIL
LINGER	ALACRITY	DISMAYED	INSINUATING	WOOED
BOMBAST	FIE	FREE SPACE	EGREGIOUSLY	CONSPIRE
BAWDY	SUBORNED	PROMULGATE	REPROACH	PERDITION
ANON	OBSEQUIOUS	INCONTINENT	PREFERMENT	MARS

Othello Vocabulary

BASE	CREDULOUS	EXPOSTULATE	REQUISITES	CASTIGATION
BEGUILED	TEMPEST	TRIFLE	SATIETY	SHRIFT
LASCIVIOUS	IMPEDIMENT	FREE SPACE	SURFEITED	DELUDING
MANDATE	GRATIFY	MALICE	GRANGE	MARS
PREFERMENT	INCONTINENT	OBSEQUIOUS	ANON	PERDITION

Othello Vocabulary

PERIL	SHRIFT	FIE	BASE	MARS
ALACRITY	INIQUITY	REQUISITES	REPROACH	ADVOCATION
IMPEDIMENT	CREDULOUS	FREE SPACE	GRATIFY	INSINUATING
DISMAYED	PERNICIOUS	WIT	PROMULGATE	SURFEITED
CONSPIRE	LINGER	TEMPEST	BAWDY	LASCIVIOUS

Othello Vocabulary

INCONTINENT	EXPOSTULATE	EGREGIOUSLY	PREFERMENT	MALICE
BESEECH	MANDATE	SATIETY	SUBORNED	BEGUILED
PERDITION	CASTIGATION	FREE SPACE	BOMBAST	IMPORTUNITY
ANON	TRIFLE	DELUDING	WOOED	LASCIVIOUS
BAWDY	TEMPEST	LINGER	CONSPIRE	SURFEITED

Othello Vocabulary

INIQUITY	CREDULOUS	GRATIFY	LINGER	CONSPIRE
MARS	SUBORNED	MALICE	DISMAYED	GRANGE
PERIL	BAWDY	FREE SPACE	BOMBAST	TEMPEST
BEGUILED	ADVOCATION	IMPORTUNITY	PROMULGATE	EXPOSTULATE
PREFERMENT	INSINUATING	ALACRITY	REPROACH	WOOED

Othello Vocabulary

IMPEDIMENT	BASE	PERDITION	PERNICIOUS	ANON
SATIETY	LASCIVIOUS	FIE	TRIFLE	EGREGIOUSLY
MANDATE	REQUISITES	FREE SPACE	DELUDING	WIT
BESEECH	SURFEITED	OBSEQUIOUS	INCONTINENT	WOOED
REPROACH	ALACRITY	INSINUATING	PREFERMENT	EXPOSTULATE

Othello Vocabulary

MALICE	SHRIFT	INCONTINENT	GRATIFY	REPROACH
ADVOCATION	SUBORNED	BESEECH	WOOED	EGREGIOUSLY
LASCIVIOUS	TEMPEST	FREE SPACE	MARS	TRIFLE
PERDITION	IMPEDIMENT	EXPOSTULATE	DISMAYED	ALACRITY
PERNICIOUS	INSINUATING	SATIETY	BAWDY	REQUISITES

Othello Vocabulary

CREDULOUS	INIQUITY	MANDATE	BOMBAST	BEGUILED
CASTIGATION	ANON	BASE	LINGER	DELUDING
GRANGE	PERIL	FREE SPACE	OBSEQUIOUS	PROMULGATE
FIE	SURFEITED	CONSPIRE	IMPORTUNITY	REQUISITES
BAWDY	SATIETY	INSINUATING	PERNICIOUS	ALACRITY

Othello Vocabulary

BESEECH	GRATIFY	BAWDY	CASTIGATION	PROMULGATE
GRANGE	IMPORTUNITY	CONSPIRE	FIE	WIT
LASCIVIOUS	MALICE	FREE SPACE	ANON	INIQUITY
TEMPEST	PERNICIOUS	OBSEQUIOUS	SATIETY	TRIFLE
MARS	REQUISITES	EXPOSTULATE	MANDATE	BASE

Othello Vocabulary

DELUDING	INCONTINENT	PERIL	REPROACH	CREDULOUS
WOOED	PREFERMENT	IMPEDIMENT	LINGER	PERDITION
ADVOCATION	BEGUILED	FREE SPACE	DISMAYED	SURFEITED
SHRIFT	ALACRITY	EGREGIOUSLY	BOMBAST	BASE
MANDATE	EXPOSTULATE	REQUISITES	MARS	TRIFLE

Othello Vocabulary

TEMPEST	ALACRITY	MARS	BAWDY	CONSPIRE
IMPORTUNITY	BESEECH	MANDATE	BOMBAST	SATIETY
PROMULGATE	ADVOCATION	FREE SPACE	BASE	WOOED
SUBORNED	GRANGE	PERNICIOUS	EXPOSTULATE	REQUISITES
CREDULOUS	IMPEDIMENT	OBSEQUIOUS	DISMAYED	INCONTINENT

Othello Vocabulary

INSINUATING	EGREGIOUSLY	SHRIFT	MALICE	PERDITION
LASCIVIOUS	REPROACH	TRIFLE	PREFERMENT	FIE
WIT	GRATIFY	FREE SPACE	LINGER	ANON
PERIL	CASTIGATION	DELUDING	SURFEITED	INCONTINENT
DISMAYED	OBSEQUIOUS	IMPEDIMENT	CREDULOUS	REQUISITES

Othello Vocabulary

BESEECH	WIT	REQUISITES	BASE	PERNICIOUS
ADVOCATION	MANDATE	BOMBAST	OBSEQUIOUS	CONSPIRE
LINGER	DISMAYED	FREE SPACE	TRIFLE	TEMPEST
IMPEDIMENT	DELUDING	EGREGIOUSLY	SATIETY	FIE
ANON	ALACRITY	GRANGE	BEGUILED	INCONTINENT

Othello Vocabulary

SURFEITED	PERIL	SUBORNED	SHRIFT	IMPORTUNITY
GRATIFY	WOOED	INSINUATING	LASCIVIOUS	PROMULGATE
BAWDY	INIQUITY	FREE SPACE	CREDULOUS	EXPOSTULATE
PREFERMENT	MALICE	MARS	REPROACH	INCONTINENT
BEGUILED	GRANGE	ALACRITY	ANON	FIE

Othello Vocabulary

FIE	CONSPIRE	IMPEDIMENT	CASTIGATION	ADVOCATION
BOMBAST	TEMPEST	GRATIFY	BESEECH	EGREGIOUSLY
MARS	DISMAYED	FREE SPACE	TRIFLE	INCONTINENT
PREFERMENT	LASCIVIOUS	PERIL	SATIETY	PERDITION
MANDATE	BASE	SURFEITED	EXPOSTULATE	INSINUATING

Othello Vocabulary

ALACRITY	OBSEQUIOUS	WOOED	SHRIFT	MALICE
CREDULOUS	ANON	PERNICIOUS	INIQUITY	DELUDING
GRANGE	WIT	FREE SPACE	BAWDY	REQUISITES
PROMULGATE	LINGER	BEGUILED	SUBORNED	INSINUATING
EXPOSTULATE	SURFEITED	BASE	MANDATE	PERDITION

Othello Vocabulary

DISMAYED	MALICE	SURFEITED	PERDITION	IMPORTUNITY
PREFERMENT	WOOED	OBSEQUIOUS	SUBORNED	ALACRITY
TEMPEST	PERIL	FREE SPACE	BOMBAST	MARS
DELUDING	CREDULOUS	SATIETY	MANDATE	WIT
SHRIFT	REQUISITES	IMPEDIMENT	BEGUILED	FIE

Othello Vocabulary

CASTIGATION	INCONTINENT	LASCIVIOUS	PERNICIOUS	BAWDY
INSINUATING	LINGER	PROMULGATE	EGREGIOUSLY	TRIFLE
GRANGE	ADVOCATION	FREE SPACE	GRATIFY	BASE
ANON	BESEECH	CONSPIRE	REPROACH	FIE
BEGUILED	IMPEDIMENT	REQUISITES	SHRIFT	WIT

www.ingramcontent.com/pod-product-compliance
Lightning Source LLC
Chambersburg PA
CBHW081457070526
44586CB00019B/2394